THE DRAMATIC LITERATURE OF NAWAL EL SAADAWI

Nawal El Saadawi

The Dramatic Literature
of Nawal El Saadawi

Edited by
Adele S. Newson-Horst

Isis
Translated from the Arabic by
Rihab Kassatly Bagnole

God Resigns at the Summit Meeting
Translated from the Arabic by
Sherif Hetata

SAQI

London   San Francisco   Beirut

ISBN: 978-0-86356-683-7

First published by Saqi, London 2009

A full CIP record for this book is available from the British Library.
A full CIP record for this book is available from the Library of Congress.

Manufactured in Lebanon

SAQI

26 Westbourne Grove, London W2 5RH
825 Page Street, Suite 203, Berkeley, California 94710
Tabet Building, Mneimneh Street, Hamra, Beirut

www.saqibooks.com

Table of Contents

Acknowledgments

I would like to thank the author, Nawal El Saadawi, for the courageous efforts she advanced in writing the two plays contained in this volume. Saadawi writes what she believes and makes no excuses for her beliefs. Yet, refreshingly, her beliefs are open to debate.

I would also like to thank André Gaspard, the publisher of Saqi Books, for his enthusiasm for this project. Gaspard has a distinguished history of support for the voices of creative writers. Saqi has published and continues to publish many of El Saadawi's works, including *Two Women in One*, *Love in the Kingdom of Oil*, and *The Fall of the Imam*, among others. In a recent conversation on the rise of fundamentalism around the world, Gaspard observed, the "courageous artist consistently risks his/her own personal well-being." To which El Saadawi answered, "Democracy is a tool. Not a key. You have to prepare and make sacrifices to enjoy its fruits."

To Rihab Kassatly Bagnole (Ohio University) for her introduction to *Isis*, translations and summaries; to Jane Plastow (Leeds University) for her introduction to *God Resigns at the Summit Meeting*; and to Sherif Hetata for his translation of *God Resigns at the Summit Meeting*, I also offer heartfelt thanks for their efforts and dedication to this project.

Finally, I wish to thank Christopher J. Herr (Missouri State University) for his honest criticism and enthusiasm as well as my graduate assistant Jessica Glover for her care and attention to detail.

Adele S. Newson-Horst
June 2008

In the Light of a Liberating Female Gaze: The Dramatic Literature of Nawal El Saadawi

Nawal El Saadawi has to her credit seven dramatic works published in Arabic by Madbouli Publishers. Part of a larger series of works, these plays are: *Isis, God Resigns at the Summit Meeting, Children Singing for Love, Twelve Women in a Cell, The Torn Picture, The Ruler in the Name of God,* and *The Blue Female.* In his introduction to the series, the publisher wrote, "In the past fifty years Dr. Nawal El Saadawi has given to her Arabic readers and Arabic thought a complete project characterized by courage in speaking her mind—discussing many issues that most of the writers are afraid to address ... Her works changed the mentality of our region." *Twelve Women in a Cell* was also published in English (in the volume *Plays by Mediterranean Women*) in 1994. In the introduction to that volume, Marion Baraitser explained, "These plays allow us to reverse the position [of women] and lift the veil on ancient civilizations—Jewish, Muslim and Christian—and view them in the light of a liberating female gaze".[1] These words resonate with El Saadawi's efforts in this present volume.

Reminiscent of the early years during which El Saadawi discovers her passion for and the possibilities inherent in drama, this collection contains two plays that center on the question of the dissolution of feminine power. They can therefore be seen as works of recovery. The first dramatic work, *Isis,* was written in Cairo in 1986 after El Saadawi

saw a play by Tawfiq al-Hakim with the same title. Rihab Kassatly Bagnole recently translated it into English. The second play, *God Resigns at
the Summit Meeting*, was written in Durham, North Carolina in 1996
while she was a visiting professor at Duke University. It was translated
and edited by Sherif Hetata. *Isis* was adapted to the theater in French
and performed in Brussels in November 2007.

Many of the themes in her works of fiction and non-fiction culminate
in these two dramatic works. El Saadawi's polemics center on a debate
about justice. In her polemic justice does not exist without equality—
equality for the poor, women, and the lower economic classes. Additionally, when there is unity among these factions, as advocated in her play
Isis, the rule of the unjust or the privileged class can be defeated.

The goddess Isis appears to be El Saadawi's "personal muse" suggest-
ing the strength of and possibilities for women. In her autobiography *A
Daughter of Isis* (1999), her mother is likened to the goddess. El Saadawi
writes that her mother made her childhood happy, yet, there were times
when she felt disappointment and:

> Then something would come along and wipe it all away, delete
> it from my memory, banish it from history. My mother would
> be at her best, once more a shining star, the real mother that I
> knew, her head held high, a woman full of pride, a goddess like
> Isis, a halo of light around her head, like a full moon, a silvery
> crown that the ancient Egyptian goddess wore above her brow.
> When I watched her move it taught me to be proud, to dream
> of better things, of a place for myself in this vast world.[2]

El Saadawi appropriates Isis's legendary place in Egyptian consciousness
to enable her successes and well-being. Also in El Saadawi's poetics Isis
is associated with the arts—music, song, and dance. At the age of nine,
rather than imagining herself as a doctor, El Saadawi dreamt of sitting
at a piano playing music, singing, and/or dancing, "my feet beating on
the ground, my head crowned with the disc of the sun, lifting it up like
the goddess Isis".[3] While attending the English language school, she was

"singled ... out from all the girls to play the role of Isis on the stage".[4] Her performance was such a success that after that, whenever people saw her on the streets they would point her out and say, "There is Isis".[5]

In December 2006, Madbouli Publishers in Cairo re-issued many of her books and published for the first time *God Resigns at the Summit Meeting* in Arabic. It caused quite a stir in the Islamic world. Without reading the work, officials declared that God cannot resign and that her work constituted heresy. The police went to the publisher and ordered him to destroy all the copies of the play and he obeyed to thwart persecution. Subsequently, El Azhar leveled heresy and apostasy charges against her because of the play *God Resigns at the Summit Meeting*.

Having survived several repressive regimes, El Saadawi firmly situates herself as a writer for social justice. She insists that it is her job, as a writer, to expose the truth about colonial rule, political patrimony, and religious fundamentalism. "If I don't tell the truth," she advises with great conviction, "I don't deserve to be called a writer".[6] And writing for El Saadawi is essential because it assures that important issues, issues regarding the inequity of power and humanity, do not disappear in the shroud of propaganda that characterizes much of the world's affairs—both religious and secular.[7]

Isis, the feminine archetype for creation, is a perennial favorite for El Saadawi. Her autobiography *A Daughter of Isis* is aptly named in that Isis is the enabler of El Saadawi's resistance to domination. Similarly, in her work *Love in the Kingdom of Oil* (1993 in Arabic), a female archaeologist "goes missing with chisel" in search of proof of the existence of female goddesses. For without such proof, there can be no equality among the sexes. The high degree of male domination in the Kingdom is suggested by the fact that the protagonist has to have a written document approving her leave from either a boss or a husband. In her introduction to the play *Isis* El Saadawi explains:

> Many writers have written about Isis, the ancient Egyptian
> goddess, but no one credits her as a teacher and inventor of

agriculture, bread making, and writing, nor do they portray her accurately as a figure who had a philosophy, values, and religion. Her cult had spread her teachings in Egypt and in Europe and survived all kinds of opposition until the sixth century.

Many writers have ignored this truth about Isis and considered her merely the wife of Osiris. They have formed a mundane image of her based on her loyalty to her husband and her role as a mother. An example of such a portrayal is her role in the play *Isis*, written by Tawfiq al-Hakim, in which he limits the character of Isis to that of a woman who lost her husband and is determined to bring him back. Al-Hakim compares Isis to Sheherezade and Penelope, who also supported their husbands. He transforms Isis into a silent figure unable to participate in the debates among philosophers and writers and ready to forfeit her values for the sake of her husband.

Presented in two acts, *Isis* is the precursor to *God Resigns at the Summit Meeting*. The spirit of debate (that would lead to a functional democracy) is introduced in the play *Isis*, and it is embodied in the title character. Then in *God Resigns,* debate is central to the resolution of the myriad problems, appropriated masterfully by the female characters and culminating in a work of literature. *Isis* answers the question of how women became powerless and *God Resigns* answers the question of how, centuries later, women might regain their foothold while acknowledging the consequences of dissident acts.

Isis begins with the overthrow of the female goddess Nut and the establishment of a new world order, an "era of supreme men, the era of masculinity, the era of strong male rulers. Gone is the period of women and weak men." Ra proclaims himself the ruler of the sky and Seth, Isis's brother, the ruler of earth. To gain this seat on earth, Seth must murder Osiris, Isis's husband and his older brother. Ra's doctrine has three principles: First, he is the one and only god; there can be no others. Second, doubters of his supremacy will be eliminated. And, third, only a son may inherit the throne after him; there will be no sharing of inheritance with daughters.

After totally dissolving female power, in a scene that echoes King Shahryar's response to his beloved wife's betrayal, Ra discovers his wife's infidelity with an Ethiopian slave, and with the help of his high priest, stumbles upon the idea of female excision and the castration of slaves who are privy to Ra's harem. In this scene, El Saadawi brilliantly demonstrates female circumcision's lack of connection with religion (especially Islam); the idea for female genital mutilation was motivated by control of women—the suppression of their sexual desires. El Saadawi, then, exposes the prevalent cultural patrimony and religious fundamentalism engenders the practices.

Yet, in spite of the destruction of temples to other gods and goddesses (especially the temples of Isis) and the proclamation to destroy their images as well as their place in history, people persisted in their belief in Isis as a symbol of mercy, intelligence, and justice. She resurrects her dead husband Osiris in the form of a sailor and bears a son, Horus. They live in a poor village where all work (peasants, gods, and goddesses alike), and priests are not deemed sacred or worthy of sacrifices. When Seth discovers them, Isis rallies the people and convenes a people's court to judge Seth's crimes. Seth maintains that the fundamental issue is Isis's adultery, while Isis maintains that the issue is Seth's brutality and lack of honor. Honor she equates with justice.

In the one-act play, *God Resigns at the Summit Meeting*, the prophets and the great women go to the mountain, where God is believed to reside, to request His help. Moses' people have turned from God to pursue wealth. Jesus is plagued by the queries of demanding feminists. Muhammad has to contend with corrupt Arab governments. And, Satan wishes to tender his resignation.

God grants an audience with the prophets, the great women, Satan, and various other characters and emissaries—including Bill Clinton and then Prime Minister of Israel Benjamin Netanyahu. The meeting is characterized by dozens of opposing viewpoints and the exhortations of injustice by Bint Allah, daughter of God, who is also, ironically, a writer. In El Saadawi's cosmology, writers are often in collusion with the status quo. This stifles their creativity and renders them artistically impotent. Unlike the so-called great writer in her work *The Fall of the Imam*, Bint Allah does not suffer this malaise.

God suggests a closed meeting with His prophets and emissaries—all men. The great women object, but the closed meeting is held in spite of the objection. The goal of the closed meeting (even though God's entrance is followed by, among others, representatives of the press and television) is to permit "an exchange between Him and His benevolent emissaries concerning problems affecting the universe."

First, they attempt to find a replacement for Satan among their lot. Second, they attempt to elect a new prophet to set the world right. They are unable to affect either of the goals and send for the great women of history to help. In the end, God resigns and Bint Allah is arrested for a play that she writes.

Why do these two works take the form of dramatic literature to recover the power of women in history? The basic driving force in both plays is the clash of ideas as they address women. Thursday nights at the boarding school, Helwan Secondary School for Girls, El Saadawi entertained her classmates by writing and acting out plays. *Adam Bede* was among the English language novels assigned to her. The story of a woman becoming pregnant with an illegitimate baby reminded her "of the servant-girl Shalabeya, who had worked in my late grandfather's house, and this suggested itself to me as a play which I then wrote under the title *A Scream in the Night*".[8] When the headmistress discovered evidence of the play, El Saadawi was nearly expelled and the discovery marked the end of the so-called Freedom Theatre she had run.[9] Like *A Scream in the Night*, El Saadawi believes that the tragedies of life lend themselves best to dramatic performance. Perhaps this lesson was learned as a result of her lead in the play *Isis* as a young girl of nine. The effects of her performance remained with her audience long afterwards.

The title of the little theatre suggests that the performance of tragedies lead to freedom.

Additionally, the fruits of debate are found in drama. Isis, Seth tells Ra, is a great debater who was encouraged by their mother Nut. In *God Resigns* Jesus is plagued by the questions of feminists. In a totalitarian regime there can be no debate. Yet it is the spirit of true debate that creates the dramatic tension in the two works, and it is also the spirit of debate that El Saadawi believes will result in true democracy, characteristic of wide participation. In literature, she explains, the brain was created when the character walked out of the chorus and started to speak alone. In other words, like Eve who chose knowledge, debate is essential to an enlightened existence.

Additionally, female characterization in both works is complex and thoroughly drawn around creative evocations of their imagined lives. El Saadawi's Isis is alternately fierce, vain, confident, strong, and merciful. In act one, scene three, she appears as maliciously unrelenting and brutal as Seth. This strongly contrasts with the image of Isis the loving wife in Tawfiq al-Hakim's *Isis*. Finally, in both works, the world order is suspiciously similar to El Saadawi's description of the modern world: "we are dominated or governed by one global system which is now called the New World Order".[10] She goes on to warn that:

> If capitalist relations continue to govern the major part of our world, must it be the most aggressive and reactionary forces that hold the upper hand, those built on war, on military production, on the arms race, on racial, ethnic, sexual and religious discrimination, on destruction of the natural environment, pollution and imbalance of the ecosystem, on master-slave relations between countries and peoples of the South [the so-called developing world] and countries and peoples of the North [the so-called first world]?[11]

In *God Resigns*, Bint Allah (the daughter of God), whom many readers will liken to the author herself, is unrelenting in her pursuit of justice—holding the three Holy Books, God, and the Prophets up to a standard of religious justice El Saadawi learned from her paternal grandmother. Bint Allah is entirely a creation of El Saadawi. She first appears in the novel *The Fall of the Imam* and is the illegitimate daughter of the Imam. In this work, Bint Allah conspires with the Legal Wife of the Imam (a westerner) and her mother Gawaher (the prostitute) to effect the fall of the representative of God on earth using reason and a refusal to allow male possession of their minds. The character Bint Allah in the play *God Resigns at the Summit Meeting* is described as "a girl eighteen years old who resembles Eve and looks as though she could be her daughter. But her hair is cut short and on her feet she wears a pair of dancing shoes. She steps lightly over the ground and sometimes dances. Her dress is short above her knees." She is as fierce and audacious as El Saadawi herself. As Jane Plastow points out in her introduction to *God Resigns*, "The idea of Allah having a daughter is both transgressive and teasing—a beautiful counterpart to Christ as the son of God." And, the character is an imaginative representation of which Satan approves. Which stands to reason, since in El Saadawi's poetics, Satan is the original seeker of knowledge reserved only for God. El Saadawi describes the Devil as "the first rebel in history, the only angel who questioned what the other angels feared to question and the only one that tried to see things from a different perspective".[12] And at the heart of *God Resigns* is the question of perspective.

Additionally, Eve's attempt to re-insert herself in the Holy Books, to redefine her seminal act as "the first to lead the human race to knowledge and not death," and her subsequent questioning of God's will and intent offer resoundingly compelling arguments.

Common to both works is a call for democracy—the participation of those who have been disenfranchised. Isis mobilizes the peasants and slaves while Bint Allah calls for broad participation in the summit. The exposure to broad participation is rendered in the play Bint Allah writes and for which she is imprisoned. Literature, then, becomes a tool for social justice.

Rihab Kassatly Bagnole and Jane Plastow offer added insight into the two dramatic works with introductions to *Isis* and *God Resigns*, respectively. Bagnole is a young Middle Eastern academic who finds in El Saadawi's *Isis* more than a correction of history: "She attempted to reassess what had been set out before her. Of course, it is expected of Nawal El Saadawi that she would reform inconsistencies and introduce truths because she is a woman who dares." Plastow, both an academic and theater practitioner, dubs *God Resigns at the Summit Meeting* "an epic platonic debate of play where Nawal El Saadawi finally brings all her thinking about monotheistic religion as an oppressive construct together." Their observations continue and elaborate on the debate.

Adele S. Newson-Horst

Notes

1.   Marion Baraitser, ed., *Plays by Mediterranean Women*, p. 4.
2.   El Saadawi, *A Daughter of Isis: The Autobiography of Nawal El Saadawi*, London: Zed Books, 1999, p. 4.
3.   Ibid., p. 100.
4.   Ibid., p. 101.
5.   Ibid., p. 101.
6.   Adele Newson-Horst, 'Conversations with Nawal El Saadawi', in *World Literature Today*, 82:1, January–February 2008, p. 55.
7.   Ibid., p. 55.
8.   *A Daughter of Isis*, p. 219.
9.   Ibid., p. 221.
10.   *The Nawal El Saadawi Reader,* London: Zed Books, 1997, p. 12.
11.   Ibid., p. 30.
12.   'The Seventh International AWSA Conference: Rationale and the Way Forward', *Meridians: Feminism, Race, Transnationalism,* 6:2, November 2, 2006, p. 24.

Works Cited

Baraitser, Marion (editor), *Plays by Mediterranean Women*, London: Aurora Metro Publications, 1994.

Newson-Horst, Adele, "Conversations with Nawal El Saadawi", *World Literature Today*, 82:1, January–February 2008, pp. 55–58.

El Saadawi, Nawal, *A Daughter of Isis: The Autobiography of Nawal El Saadawi*, London: Zed Books, 1999.

—*The Fall of the Imam*, London: Saqi, 2002.

—*The Nawal El Saadawi Reader*, London: Zed Books, 1997.

—The Seventh International AWSA Conference: Rationale and the Way Forward, *Meridians: Feminism, Race, Transnationalism*, 6:2, November 2, 2006, pp. 22–32.

—The Introduction to *Isis*, translated by Rihab Bagnole.

ISIS

A Play in Two Acts

Introduction

In her introduction to *Isis* (1986), Nawal El Saadawi explains, "This play, which I am presenting now, is the Egyptian Isis as I understand her from history. History belongs to everyone who possesses an amount of imagination, brains, and a genuine curiosity to know the truth." This declaration sparked my curiosity (as an Arab woman and an American educator) to investigate how a writer from the same region as mine might reinterpret history. What I discovered after reading *Isis* was, no, El Saadawi did not correct history; she attempted to reassess what had been set out before her. Of course, it is expected of Nawal El Saadawi that she would reform inconsistencies and introduce truths because she is a woman who dares.

I met Nawal El Saadawi at The Spring Literary Festival at Ohio University in 2007, but I knew about her from her writings three decades earlier, while I was still a student at the University of Damascus in Syria in the 1970s. Who back then could resist reading *Memoir of a Woman Doctor* (1958), *Women and Sex* (1972), and *The Naked Face of Arab Women* (1974), the marvelous early books of Nawal El Saadawi? Her topics appealed to my generation because they discussed taboo subjects that we were eager to explore, and they taught us the secrets of femininity and the importance of self-appreciation. We could not put down a book by Nawal El Saadawi once we started reading it and my group of friends and I used to hide *Women and Sex* inside a textbook to read without interruption.

Parents and teachers monitored the activities of their youths and kept a close eye on their behaviors; therefore, we did not want to be caught red-handed with illicit material. Reading provocative literature would attract attention to our rebellious nature, demonstrating our awareness of forbidden subjects, which would, consequently, affect our privileges. Accordingly, these books became precious items for their content. In this regard, we depended on El Saadawi to educate and unify young people who wanted to learn, investigate, and grasp the potential of their bodies and illuminate their minds. It is also important to mention that books by Nawal El Saadawi were not restricted to female readers. My introduction to these books actually came about through my older brother, Bassam, who suggested *Women and Sex* after he had read it. I considered him my best friend and intellectual advisor, someone who inspired me to read classics such as *The Iliad* and *The Odyssey*, *Don Quixote*, *The Three Musketeers*, and *Madame de Bovary*, and whom I witnessed engaging in night-long debates with a group of passionate friends in spontaneous discussions about all kinds of interesting topics. It was among these friends that we were able to exchange the most interesting books and my copy of *Women and Sex* ended up with the sister of another member of this enthusiastic group.

I was also interested in the literature about ancient Mediterranean deities, a topic that was not commonly discussed in Islamic cultures and for which resources were rare. In most cases, the topic of ancient goddesses and gods was broached to highlight and reinforce the relevance of the prevailing religions of Christianity, Islam, and—to a certain degree—Judaism (which were not emphasized due to the conflict with Israel) as a means of saving our species from the destruction and harm of previous religions. I must note that recently some countries in the Middle East have started to acknowledge the importance of ancient deities to their history and started employing their own autochthonous resources to encourage research about their heritage, attract tourism, and boost their economies. For example, in 1990, the first national Syrian theatrical dance company was established under the name of the ancient Syrian moon goddess of love, fertility, and art: Enana. Of course, utilizing the name of this goddess for a contemporary purpose restores her honor and acknowledges her importance to the indigenous culture. This is an audacious choice and the president, Bashar al-Assad, who was educated in Western universities and is not a conservative Muslim, permitted the dance group to perform under the banner of the goddess. Earlier on, only writings of a historical nature or those prompting a moral lesson discussed the ancient deities and were locally accessible. For example, *Isis* by Tawfiq al-Hakim (1955) was available because it did not honor Isis as a goddess, but as a wife and mother. Her role is presented as that of a faithful woman who is there to ensure the happiness and continuity of her husband's name. She has to sacrifice her needs and all her possessions for her husband and his well-being. She is also dedicated to raising his children and teaching them how to become good citizens.

The representation of Isis as a caring mother was a common motif in ancient Egypt. She appeared as a divine figure nursing or holding her child in many of her statues. Her figure was carved full-length, standing or seated in ancient temples or in relief on the walls of sacred places. Nowadays, statues of Isis appear in museums around the world, revealing the skills and aesthetics of those who believed in her in ancient times. For example, a small faience statue of Isis (300–30 BC) was part of the special exhibition entitled "The Art of Medicine in Ancient Egypt" (September 13, 2005 to May 7, 2006) in the Metropolitan Museum of Art in New York City, and another large basalt statue (1300 BC) is part of the permanent collection in the Egyptian Museum in Cairo. Although the religious role of Isis as the goddess of healing, salvation, and fertility perished completely with the spread of Christianity, her fundamental role as representation of beauty, order, and culture has never ceased.

Isis, Nephthys, Seth, and Osiris were the children of Nut, the goddess of the heavens, and Geb, the god of earth. According to the myth, Isis's marriage to her brother, Osiris, angered Seth. Seth tricked Osiris into lying in a coffin, then sealed it and discarded it in the River Nile. Isis searched and found the coffin, warmed the body of her husband, returned him to life, and subsequently gave birth to their son, Horus. Seth avenged this act by cutting Osiris into pieces and dispersing his remains around Egypt. Isis found and gathered all the parts of her husband except his sex organ, which was swallowed by a fish. Isis then made a mold of the missing part and, with the help of Horus, ensured Osiris's eternal life. The cult of Isis spread from Alexandria throughout the Hellenistic and Roman world around the fourth century BC. She was worshiped with Osiris and Horus, identified with other Greek goddesses such as Demeter and Aphrodite, and had a cult of her own. Worship in her temples effectively vanished, like all cults associated with the goddesses, in the early centuries of the Common Era. However, interest in Isis and other goddesses was revived when women became more aggressive in searching for their own history, demanding their rights, and pursuing equality through the feminist movement of the twentieth century.

Some feminist artists and writers used the imagery of the goddess as a symbol of empowerment and an emblem of achievement. For example, the American artist Judy Chicago evoked many ancient goddesses in her renowned installation, "The Dinner Party" (first exhibited in 1979). On the other side of the globe, El Saadawi was studying and researching the ancient deities of the region for an entirely different artistic medium. Naturally, she drew on the goddess of her own background to use as an effective heroine when she was contemplating a new play. Incidentally, the goddess in the play is not only a character but also part of the writer's history and a figure familiar to her intended readers, and so the play is called: *Isis* (published in 1984 in Arabic).

I did not read *Isis* by Nawal El Saadawi until after I met the writer in the spring of 2007. In fact, I did not even know about the play. During one of our conversations about dance and theater, El Saadawi mentioned *Isis* and gave me a photocopy of the play in Arabic. When she expressed her intention to have it translated, I decided to take on the challenge. My enthusiasm for the work was based not only on my joint admiration for the writer El Saadawi and the goddess *Isis*, but also for the chosen artistic medium common in ritual worshipping. The play, which will eventually become a performance, is the most suitable and richest medium for a deity like Isis because it presents her in her ceremonial setting. Deities and performance have often been linked together since humans created them and endowed them with special powers. Thus, we read about a pre-dynastic Egyptian Amration goddess performing her prayers with arms raised in adoration, an ancient Minoan serpent-worshipping goddess revealing herself holding snakes in her bare hands, and many other performances of ancient religions, including Christianity, as part of worship rituals. Such performances were intended to fascinate the community, impress the deities, and strengthen the faith in the heart of the believer through a renewal of their relationship to the deities in question.

Isis is not only a play about a great goddess of the ancient world. It is a contemporary presentation of the many discriminating rules that control the daughters of Isis. It tells about the present leaders of the lands of Isis who refuse to grant women their basic rights and have transformed them into second-class citizens. These women suffer physical mutilation, violation, and mental manipulation by self-assigned protectors who fear women's sexuality and are threatened by their freedom. Under the banner of honor, these patriarchal societies assign men the right to discipline women and denounce their infidelity. Thus, women and their children are unprotected and unable to seek justice in their homelands because the religious and secular laws of their cultures do not validate them as rational beings and there are no laws to secure their rights and safety.

Isis is also about men and masculinity. It tells about honest and compassionate men who may end up tortured, stripped of their pride, or assassinated by greedy and power-hungry groups. These immoral bands of men legitimize their rulings by soliciting support from the army and religious groups who back their illegitimate rulings. Eventually these corrupt rulers lose power in the lands of Isis because her children realize their wickedness. In this regard, *Isis* is also about hope for better governments and laws that grant women equal rights and allow them to become contributors and decision-makers in matters that will benefit them and their children and steer their societies in the right directions. This will come about through determination, solidarity, and the continuous struggle for equal rights.

When I decided to translate *Isis* I read it several times to familiarize myself with its patterns, style, and methods, to plan an approach suitable for keeping the spirit of the English version true to the original. I noticed that Nawal El Saadawi wrote *Isis* in a combination of standard and colloquial Egyptian Arabic. She also repeated words and sentences in the dialogue to emphasize an idea—a style known in informal conversation among Arabic speakers. Therefore, the combination of these elements makes the play easily comprehensible to a variety of readers because it is true to the nature of their own verbal communication. Accordingly, it is important to keep the spirit of the play intact and convey the writer's intention to transmit her background and those of the characters accurately. I was aware that some Arabic words must be interpreted, rather than translated, because they do not have an exact match in English. I used words that through their connotations suggest the state of achievement and the environment of the time. *Isis* is divided into two acts with each act comprising six scenes. It starts out with power in the hands of the gods Ra and Seth, who are deciding who rules the people, and the play ends with power in the hands of the people. With the help of the female goddess, the people regain their power and start living a happier life. I hope that the reader of this translation will also believe in the collective power of women to change the world into a better place for women, their families, and their countries.

As a daughter of Isis, I strongly feel that by translating *Isis* I am paying homage to my ancestors, who believed in the power of this goddess, and expressing my gratitude to her for helping those individuals when they prayed to her. I also extend my appreciation to Nawal El Saadawi for her bravery in speaking out for Middle Eastern women who have been trying to regain their rights in repressive cultures. Therefore, my endeavor is partly ritualistic and partly a contribution to the mission of empowering all like-minded women around the world. The translator hopes that this English version of *Isis* will help readers to discover the true meaning of the goddess Isis as intended by its writer, Nawal El Saadawi. I hope that this labor of love and friendship will assist women all over the world in their voyage towards equality and a better life.

Rihab Kassatly Bagnole

Cast

Characters in order of appearance
Ra
Seth
Isis
Maat
Peasant Mother
Army Chief
Sailor / Osiris
Horus
Priest
Child 1
Child 2
Child 3
High Priest
Slave
Tut
Masta
Priest / Court Leader
Chorus
Villagers, both men & women
Girls in harem
Entourage of Ra
Slaves
Soldiers
Merchants, artisans, writers, et al, poor

ACT ONE

SCENE ONE

The god Ra is sitting on his throne in the sky where he has summoned Seth to attend him after his triumph in a battle.

In the presence of Ra, Seth is wearing a dagger.

RA   You have proved to me in this last battle that you are a brave soldier. In addition to your bravery and faith in me, the sun god Ra, owner of the sky and sun, who has become the one and only god, I am certain that your heart is filled with faith in combination with your ingenuity and vigor in war. Victory cannot be achieved without faith and power. Now we are in the era of supreme men, the era of masculinity, the era of strong men rulers. Gone is the period of women and weak men.

SETH   Yes, almighty Ra.

RA   Gone is the period in which equality has spread among the weak and the strong, the sons of gods and the sons of people, men and women. We lived in a time of primitiveness and darkness, an era of numerous gods in the sky and various rulers on earth. From now on, there is only one god in the sky, the god Ra, the sun god. And there is only one ruler on earth, Geb, the god of earth.

SETH   Yes, almighty Ra, We won the battle with the power of our faith, our weapons, and men's solidarity. You seized the kingdom of the sky and my father, Geb, the kingdom of earth.

RA   I want you to ring the bells and let the megaphones and hornpipes declare me, the god Ra, victorious over Nut, goddess of the sky, who has suffered a great loss and has no place any longer in the kingdom of the sky or the earth. The era of mother Nut's authority has ended and the time of the sacred father, the almighty Ra, has just begun.

SETH   We have so declared with our megaphones and hornpipes.

RA   How did the people receive the news?

SETH   With happiness, joy, and welcome.

RA   Except women of course.

SETH   And some doubting men of weak faith.

RA   (*angry*) Being burned to death or throwing them to the animals to devour their bodies will punish them. Let all of them know that I am the god Ra, who may forgive all flaws except the flaw of skepticism and unfaithfulness. Have you announced this?

SETH   Yes.

RA   And who are those who doubt me?

SETH   You will take care of them. There is no need for you to become irate and ruin your mood, almighty god Ra.

RA   My rage is horrible and nothing can restrain it.

SETH   This is well known and natural for the almighty god.

RA   But who are they? Do you know their names?

Seth remains silent.

RA   Why are you silent? Are you hiding something from me, Seth?

SETH   No, almighty god Ra. But I will give them another chance to repent and return to the just and wise path.

RA   I have never known this sympathy from you. Are you afraid I will harm someone special to you among them?

Seth is silent.

RA   Your brother Osiris and sister Isis? Do not think I do not know what is happening on earth. It is true that my throne is above the edge of the sun in the sky, but I follow what is transpiring on earth. I know that your sister Isis and brother Osiris are among the rebels, and I would harm them but for you.

SETH My devotion to you, almighty god Ra, is above my relationship with my sister, brother, or any blood relatives. I have fought on your side against my mother, Nut, and there is no closer blood relation than the mother. I have sacrificed!

RA This is proof of your strong faith, Seth. You will be extremely rewarded for this devotion.

SETH And what is my reward, almighty god?

RA What do you want? Ask and I will grant your request at once.

SETH I want to inherit the throne of earth after my father Geb.

RA Let it be. You will be the god of earth after your father Geb. Do you want me to announce it today or postpone it till ...

He is silent for a moment.

... till your father's death. He is sick and in his last days. It is wise to wait, and it is humane as well. What is your opinion, Seth?

SETH Yes, almighty god. I can wait until my father passes away. But the wait may be long. My temperament as a man of war ... a man of war is restless by nature and cannot bear the long delay. I do not want to look like someone who is waiting for his father's death to inherit the throne. I love my father anyway, despite his lack of feeling towards me and his preference for his other offspring.

RA Do you mean Isis and Osiris?

SETH He also favored Nephthys over me. He does not say it though. On the contrary, he claims that I am the best of his children, but I feel the opposite.

RA Do you mean he lies to you?

SETH No, almighty god Ra, I do not think he lies. However, since the death of my mother, Nut, he has been suffering a schizophrenic condition between his mind and heart. He knows in his mind that I am the best of his children, his right arm and his strong limb, but he does not feel anything in his heart for me. I do not know why, although I abide by his commands and do not disobey his orders, in contrast to Isis and Osiris who do not hesitate to debate everything with him, including the sacred.

RA   (*angry*) The sacred too?

SETH   I heard them saying that everything can be argued and debated.

RA   (*angry*) They do not believe in the divinity of Ra or that my dogma is indisputable and incontestable?

SETH   They love argument and philosophy. To them, everything should be submitted to reason and assessment.

RA   (*angry*) Did they debate the rule of your mother Nut when she was the goddess of the sky?

SETH   Yes, almighty god Ra. It was not their fault. It was my mother who trained them in debate and argument and taught them that nothing was above reason and justice, including divinity.

RA   Your mother, Nut, ascended to the position of sky goddess unexpectedly. She lacked reason and her brain could not understand sacred divinity. This was the reason for her defeat and downfall from the throne.

SETH   My mother did not believe that the sky god needs the power of the sword and dagger like the god of earth. She used to say that justice is above power, and peace is above war. (*Seth draws his dagger*)

RA   It is the feminist philosophy, which is based on weakness and helplessness with swords and weapons. Your mother Nut verified her weakness by speaking about peace. She and her beliefs were severely defeated, marking the end of weak deities. If a god does not have great power in the heart to scare people, how

would they submit to him and worship him? How
would they obey him? Obedience does not survive
without terror, and terror does not exist without
strong authority and dreadful fright. Did anyone
dread your mother Nut? She used to walk among
people in the markets without admonition, an entourage, or an army, as if she were one of the humans.
Gone is that era, the era of the human gods. It is the
start of the inhumane gods. The gods who do not
walk among people in the markets and are not visible
by eye, except as heavenly rays emerging in the disc
of the sun. This is the god of the sun, the almighty
god Ra. Have you announced this to the people?

SETH Yes, yes. We announced all with the megaphones.

RA And hornpipes?

SETH The hornpipes too. And we requested that Tut
the scribe write it out too, so it is documented on
paper.[1]

RA Yes, my orders and my laws must be written down.
To instill terror the god must not stand in front of
people to give speeches. Human ears must not hear
my sacred voice. In any case, people fear and revere
the written word more. I want my words to be sacred
beyond contestation and dispute, and greater than
human intellect. Has Tut recorded all this?

SETH Yes, almighty god. All this is written and documented
in a scroll.

RA This is your holy book. Every sentence starts with my
name, god Ra the almighty, and in front of the name
a symbol in the shape of the disc of the sun.

SETH That is exactly what we have done.

RA My doctrine has three principles: First, I am the god
Ra, god of the sun, who owns all the sky, and there is
no god but I sitting on the throne of the sky.

---

1. Tut is a character based on the scribe and artist from Tawfiq al-Hakim's play *Isis*,
published in 1955 by Maktaba al-Adab in Cairo. Tut has a friend, Mastat, who is
also a scribe and musician.

SETH This is documented, almighty god.

RA The second principle: Whoever doubts the sacred quality of Ra will be burned to death or thrown to the wild animals to be devoured.

SETH This is also inscribed.

RA The third principle: I am the only one who decides which of my sons will inherit the throne of the sky after me. Only a son may inherit while the daughter has no share.

SETH Yes, this is the third principle.

RA These are the main principles in my doctrine, aren't they?

SETH Yes.

RA You can remind me if I forget anything. Great is the one who does not forget.

SETH Nothing is left except the throne of the earth.

RA The throne of earth is your father Geb's share. I gave him the designation of god of earth. Is it not enough for him? Your father was not committed with all his heart during the battle.

SETH Indeed, my father was torn between his loyalty to you and his fidelity to my mother, Nut. My mother occupied his heart. But his mind was with us.

RA Lucky for me, you did not inherit your father's weakness. Nothing undermines a man as much as his emotions and the strong man is the one who conquers his feelings and defeats them. As for a powerful god, he does not have sentiments, which is the secret of the tyranny of gods.

SETH My father was weak in front of my mother Nut and now he is vulnerable before his sons and daughters, especially Isis. He loves her and prefers her to all of us, and if the matter were in his hand, he would give her the throne.

RA I will decide this matter and not your father Geb. He must understand this clearly. I decide the successor to the throne of the sky and the earth. The successor must be a male ... a man ... and not a woman, not a female. Gone is the era of women; the era of manliness, courage, power, and fear has begun ... Your sister Isis must realize this truth and forget the past and the old epoch. As for you, Seth, you will inherit the throne of the earth after your father.

SETH   And Osiris?

RA   He has no share in the throne. He did not fight on my behalf and threw his support to his mother Nut.

SETH   He may demand his right to inherit like me.

RA   The heir is you and there will be only one heir, not two or three. Gone is the time of many rulers and authorities on earth or in the sky. Your father Geb is the only god on earth. He has no partner and you, Seth, will be his heir. I believe in oneness on earth and in the sky too.

SETH   Osiris will not be convinced of that, nor will Isis. I am afraid ...

RA   (*interrupting*) Afraid of what? Is a courageous warrior like you afraid of anything? Are you afraid of anyone when I, Ra, am with you? Do you not trust my power and authority?

SETH   I beg your pardon, almighty god. I am not afraid of anyone but the problem is complex and it will not be easy ...

RA   Is it Osiris you are afraid of?

SETH   Not Osiris, almighty god. Osiris is not a knight or a fighter. He did not train to handle a dagger like me. I will certainly defeat him. The problem is not Osiris ... the problem is Isis, almighty god.

RA   What? Are you afraid of a woman?

SETH   Isis is not a woman, almighty god.

RA   If she is not a woman, what is she then?

SETH   She is a goddess who displays on her head the crown of sacredness. She is not easily convinced and she challenges everyone.

RA   This was during the past era. Now, no one wears the

crown of sacredness in the sky or on the earth without my will, that of the god Ra. Whoever opposes my wish will be punished by death, death with this dagger.

God Ra points at the dagger in Seth's hand.

Seth bows his head in silence.

RA   Why are you silent? Is not this my doctrine?

SETH   Yes, Almighty God Ra. But. ...

RA   (*interrupting*) The word of the almighty god Ra is the word of truth and nothing exceeds it. Do you believe this?

SETH   Yes, of course.

RA   And the strong and powerful like me needs a courageous fighter like you. Is it not so?

SETH   Yes, almighty god Ra.

RA   My word is holy, but the holy word alone is not enough because war ... holy war is what assures victory to the just god over the false god and the fake goddesses. I need the holy book and the dagger together. A god cannot neglect either of them. Is it not so?

SETH   Yes, almighty god.

RA   What are you afraid of then, with my book and dagger with you?!

Seth is silent with his head bowed.

RA   I know that Osiris is your brother and you may hesitate in eliminating him if he became an obstacle in your way to the throne. Leave Osiris to me; I will take care of him if he opposes my will.

SETH   Osiris is not the problem.

RA   Isis?!

SETH   Yes.

RA   Leave her to me too.

SETH   (*frightened*) No, almighty god Ra, not Isis. I can bear if you judge Osiris to die, but not Isis ...

Seth is disturbed and pained.

I could not bear it.

RA   Why could you not bear it?

SETH   Isis is my sister.

RA   And Osiris, is he not your brother too?

SETH   Yes, but... (*Seth is silent and does not continue his sentence*)

RA   But what?

SETH   I do not know what to say, almighty god Ra. But I could not endure seeing my sister harmed or killed ... I do not want to oppose you, almighty god ... I cannot oppose you, you will have to kill me before I do that, but I cannot lose my sister Isis. She is not only my sister almighty god ...

       I ...

       He stops and mutters.

       I ... I love her.

       Seth bows to the floor and dries his sweat with his kerchief. Ra silently observes him, somewhat surprised.

RA   Seth, you seem to have inherited your father's weakness.

SETH   Forgive me, almighty god. I did not inherit my father's weakness. All the women of the world cannot move a hair on my head, but Isis is not like the women of the world ... She is something else, almighty god ... She is a sorceress.

RA   A sorceress?! Do you believe in sorcery like the common ignorant people?

SETH   No, almighty god, but ...

RA   (*interrupting*) We will not continue conversing on this subject now. I have many other issues in the kingdom of the sky and a great deal of unsolved contests between the planets ... At the moment, I have enough problems in the sky. Also, what is Geb doing? He must get down to business, and if he is sick or cannot commence to minister to his affairs of state, he should relinquish his throne to you. Yes, to you and to no one else. This is a sacred command from the almighty god Ra, and whoever defies it will be punished by death.

And now, Seth, leave at once ... I have other urgent sacred affairs.

Seth moves hesitantly towards the exit door and then backs up with heavy slow steps.

SETH   Almighty god, I beg one last favor from you.

RA   Ask for me what you want, Seth. You are the commander of my army and I cannot refuse your request.

SETH   Promise me, almighty god, that you shall not harm my sister Isis ... You can do what you want with Osiris, but not Isis. Please do not kill her. She, no matter how much she rebels against you, is only one woman and not dangerous.

RA   She is a first-class swordfighter, who uses the weapon skillfully. She also has a treacherous mind. She, in my opinion, is more dangerous than Osiris to you and me.

SETH   No, your highness. Isis will not pose a danger, especially if she is alone without the support of Osiris. He possesses her heart, and when Osiris disappears, I may take his place in her heart and thus will gain her to our side. Isis is popular among the people. Some of them still worship her. And if I succeed in bringing her to our side we will benefit a great deal.

RA   You have to deal with these issues; do not involve me in such insignificant matters.

SETH   I may need you, almighty god, only in finishing off Osiris.

RA   Can you not do that alone without me?

SETH   I need you, almighty god, to convince the people that he died of natural causes and by the will of the almighty Ra, not by my hand and my dagger.

RA   This is true. Osiris will not die except by my will and you, Seth, are only my instrument to accomplish my wish. People must understand that I am the almighty god Ra, god of the sky, and I am the only one who rules over people in life and death. Have you announced this?

SETH Yes, almighty god. No one doubts your power.

RA Now go quickly.

Seth quickly retreats towards the exit, but god Ra calls him back.

RA Before you leave, there is one more thing. I do not want anyone to know that you meet with me. People must believe that I do not appear on earth and my dwelling is in the disc of the sun. Have you announced this?

SETH Yes, of course.

RA These meetings between us are extremely secretive. No one must know and you must not murmur about them, not even to yourself in your sleep. I may visit you in your dreams and reveal messages to the people. My soul may fly around at any time and any place, so I know what is happening on earth. You must know that nothing can be hidden from me. I know your heartbeats. And I know when your heart beats fervently and when these beats increase ...

God Ra laughs and throws his head backwards.

Yes, do not think that I was not aware of your love for Isis and that she sits on the throne of your heart. No harm in that as long as she does not interfere with the matters of the sky and the earth.

Seth smiles and seems contented and pleased.

SETH Yes, almighty god Ra. She owns my heart, but I have not conquered her heart yet. I may need your holiness to possess her heart.

RA I do not have time for personal romantic problems. Try to solve your own crisis. Do not involve the almighty Ra in every big and small issue on earth because he will not have the time or energy, except for those more sacred affairs of the sky. Go now and do not waste any more of my time.

Seth performs the official salute, moving his dagger up then down and retreats quickly.

Ra alone on the stage, looking toward the sky, then to the disc of the sun, and speaks to himself.

RA   Yes, sun ... I am Ra, the sun god ... I am the only god who has won and conquered the sky ... The sun ... I am the only one ... and there is no one but me. Me ... me.

His voice echoes on the horizon, and the sun disc glows and fills the sky. Ra sees his face reflected in the disc of the sun. He laughs then guffaws while repeating with the echo of the sound:

Me ... me ... the only one ... the only one.

SCENE TWO

The stage is completely dark ... some sparse unrecognizable voices. Many feet run on the ground, then absolute silence. The sound of the megaphone announces:

Geb, the god of earth, is dead. He left his will on a folded paper in a manuscript.

His children are around him opening the manuscript.

Absolute silence.

The voice reverberates again:

In a few minutes we will read the will of Geb, the god of earth. His sons and daughters are still opening the scroll ... Isis, Osiris, Seth, Nephthys, and Horus ...They are opening the scroll ...

Absolute silence.

The sound reverberates again:

We will be reading to you the will of Geb, god of earth.

This is his last will and testament:

After my death, Geb, the god of earth, Osiris will inherit the throne after me ...

The voices of people singing:
  Osiris
  Heart of Isis ...
  Osiris
  God of wealth ...
  God of love
  God of goodness
  Sing O valley of the Nile
  Osiris
  Our king
  Osiris
  Our lover
  Osiris
  Our king
  God of wealth and goodness
  Heart of Isis, heart of Isis.

The singing of people transforms music, dance, and rhythm, to which the crowds of women and men dance.

Suddenly everything stops. Absolute silence. Absolute darkness. The steps of soldiers marching on the ground. A low muffled sound of struggle. Daggers and swords strike in the dark. Then a sharp frightening scream. The scream of Osiris before he dies calling in agony, "Isis! Isis!"

Absolute darkness. Running steps and they move faster. The crash of a body hitting the floor.

Then, absolute silence and darkness. No sound, no movement. Nothing.

Then, the sound of the megaphone announcing in a sad tone:

People. Osiris, the god of wealth, is dead, and after him his brother, Seth, has taken the throne.

The fearful scream of Isis resonates: Osiris!

The sound of her voice echoes around the stage.

Then, absolute silence and darkness.

The megaphone announces: Hail to Seth! Long live Seth!

Absolute silence. No one answers. As if the universe is asleep.

The megaphone repeats:

> In the name of the almighty god Ra, god of the sun, we announce that the new god of earth is King Seth.
> Long live King Seth.

A few voices repeat in a low sad voice: Long live King Seth.

The voices get louder and louder and the sadness in them diminishes.

The cheers transform into group singing in a voice without happiness or enthusiasm.

> King of the land, you are handsome
> Seth, light of the eye
> O our king ... O our king
> Light of the eye ...

The voice is choking ... The singing stops abruptly. Absolute darkness and silence.

Then, the voice of Isis yells loud and clear:

> Osiris ... Osiris did not die!
> Osiris lives ... lives! Lives!
> Osiris!

The echo of her voice rings in the universe. The ears of people receive it.

The voices repeat joyfully and passionately:

Osiris lives ... Osiris lives ...

And the song starts again:

Osiris, love of Isis ...
God of wealth, god of love, god of goodness
Sing, O valley of the Nile
Osiris ...
Love of Isis ...

The feet of the soldiers hit the ground, hastening here and there while the daggers and swords strike at the people.

Confusion, chaos, screams, anxiety, and people hustling, evading and running terrified.

The stage is completely vacant. The soldiers control the situation and it is now calm. Only the iron steps advance slowly, steadily, and powerfully on the ground.

The megaphone announces:

Long live King Seth. Long live!

The crowd repeats the shouts of the officers in a militaristic funereally melody:

Long live King Seth, long live! Long may he live!

SCENE THREE

In the house of Isis.
The darkness and silence of the long night.
The voice of the mother still reverberating as a slow wind, calling out: Isis, Isis.
The light slowly reveals the face of Isis, who is sitting next to her house, poorly dressed. She is firm, silent,

confident, gazing at the horizon. Maat sits close to her,
sad and silent too.
Isis moves her head as if she hears the cry.

ISIS   I hear someone calling me. It sounds like Osiris. Yes, it is his voice. His voice is still in my ear; it is calling me. Osiris did not die. He exists; he's alive.

MAAT   (*weak and desperate*) It is the sound of the wind... The sound of air is blowing in the distance.
Isis, Osiris is dead.
Osiris died. Seth killed him. We must acknowledge the truth.

ISIS   What truth, Maat, goddess of justice and order ... What truth? Do you not hear his voice?! ... Do you not hear? ... Listen.

The calling voice is gentle like the calm wind. Isis per-
ceives it but Maat does not hear it.

MAAT   I do not hear anything. It is the sound of the wind. Osiris died, Isis; the god of goodness has died; and Nut, goddess of the sky, has died; and Maat, the goddess of justice has died. No one is left but Maat ... me ... a woman ... simply a woman ... I am not a goddess anymore ... I do not have even my freedom ... and my heart is broken.

ISIS   (*annoyed*) I do not like to hear this desperate weak voice. You are still the goddess of justice. My mother Nut is still the goddess of the sky and Osiris is still the god of generosity and goodness. And I, Isis, am still the goddess Isis ...
There is no power in the sky or on earth that can defeat us as long as we do not desire to be defeated.
A human being does not suffer defeat except from within himself, Maat, so what about the deities?!

MAAT   (*distressed*) A woman is not even a human ... The god Ra to follow and obey adjudges her. Nothing is left for her but to peel onions and bear children, like rabbits and cats.

ISIS   (*angry*) I do not like to hear this pathetic desperate voice. Desperation means death and they want us dead.

MAAT   I do not see any hope on the horizon.

ISIS   As long as we live, we create hope. We are still living ... As long as we live, hope lives.

MAAT   We alone? You and I? Even my male and female writer friends left us ... Seth seduced them with money and status. There are only a few rare ones of those who have their conscience still alive. Those also are silent, afraid of the brutality of Seth. They do not do a thing except blow in the cane pipes. We must acknowledge reality and not live in delusion. And you, Isis, the goddess of reason, you cannot keep living in a delusion. The death of Osiris is real. Seth killed him. It is true. Seth has won out over us. He has succeeded with weapons, daggers, and brutality. He has prevailed by bigotry, bribery, and embezzlement. He has triumphed by all sordid means, yet he has won and we have to admit our loss and give up.

ISIS   Admitting our loss is one thing and giving up is something else. My mother, Nut, the goddess of the sky, lost but never gave up. My mother died while resisting. We must resist as well until the last breath.

MAAT   Will Seth allow us to resist? He is chasing us down everywhere and frightening those who contact us. We do not see anyone. No one visits us. No one gets close to us. Even Tut and Mastat, we have not seen any of them since the death of Osiris. Everyone is scared and they are all silent.

ISIS   And you, Maat, are you going to be silent? Are you going to be frightened?

MAAT   I will not be scared. But I am a writer and a thinker and I do not care about what Seth does. I do not care about politics. I will write on the matters of philosophy or poetry or novels ...

ISIS But you are the goddess of justice and truth. Do you not believe in justice and truth?

MAAT Faith is in my heart. Faith means love. I love justice and it is enough for me.

ISIS Love that does not lead to action is only empty emotion. The man or woman writer who does not aim for justice is nothing but a whistle blowing air in cane pipes.

MAAT I am a neutral writer, who merely reports.

ISIS When you write a word, it becomes biased. The word is an opinion. You think you are unprejudiced because you do not side with or against Seth, but in the end your impartial position turns out to be with Seth because you know that he is brutal and an assassin and you stay silent. Your silence supports him in continuing his cruelty and crimes. You are not as neutral as you may think; you are partial, on Seth's side.

You are inclined to his side in a negative, weak way. Thus, it is inclination and not neutrality.

MAAT (*angry*) No! I am not on Seth's side.

ISIS And you are not against him either.

MAAT I am against him in my heart. Every night I pray and call on the good deities to remove this tyrant from his throne.

ISIS This is the position of the weak, the powerless.

MAAT I am weak and powerless and you are too. Yet you live in a fantasy and your imagination, and you think that you are strong and capable of working miracles. You think you can resurrect Osiris after his death. Rip away this illusion and live in reality! Osiris died! Yes, died.

ISIS No, he did not die. Osiris is the god of decency and gods do not die. Goodness cannot disappear from this universe.

Osiris, the god of kindness, lives in my heart and in the heart of each decent person. Osiris is the Nile. His generosity pours out on the people and the land. Osiris lives in every green bearing tree, in every drop of dew, in every mind, in every infant's smile, and in every song.

Osiris, he is love ... He is beauty ... He is virtue ... He is serenity.

Isis hushes. Maat seems pained while wiping her tears in silence.

Silence.

MAAT   (*drying her tears*) Osiris was kindness and tranquility. Since he has disappeared my heart has not known serenity.

Isis is silent and sad.

MAAT   Seth has not had enough, Isis. He has not renounced his evil acts. He is not going to calm down until he gets you too. The only way for you now is to escape and disappear from him.

ISIS   I will not escape. I will face him with the accusation of murder. I will confront him face to face.

(*She backs up*) But I hate his face. I do not like to see him. I will not see him until all kindness has dispersed from my being. I have never loved him. He did not inspire in me anything except the feelings of hate and detestation.

In contrast to Osiris, who inspires in me the most beautiful things: love, justice, clemency, beauty, and virtue. Seth inspires the most ugly in me: anger, wickedness, and hatred. He cheats me of virtues and projects onto me his vices. The malicious traits of his face reflect themselves on my face. The feelings of anger and loathing transfer to me as if by contagion. I will not see him until the god of vice inhabits my body and mind. I do not like to see him because he makes me hate myself and my angry face in the mirror. I also hate my body when it agitates with the desire of revenge. Like a cold crawling chill … like crawling death … I loathe him like death. I wish I could grab his neck in my fingers and squeeze, squeeze, and squeeze until he takes his last breath. I do not see him in front of me, I imagine him dead by my hand, soulless. He has changed me from Isis, the kind goddess, to Isis, the destroyer.

MAAT So he wins when he inspires the devil in you. He makes you like him, convulsing with feelings of hatred and anger. He wants you to be like him. He does not want to be the sole miserable and pitiable being. He wants you like him. He aims to chase from your heart Osiris, the god of goodness and kindness. He wants to entice you to reject clemency, love, and justice. He is like the devil that cannot stand seeing the god of goodness in front of him. He cannot stand seeing his opponent face to face. And you, Isis, are the rival of Seth. Since childhood, he would break your pen and rip up your art and notebooks. And since childhood, you have been trying to change him. You have faced his malignant intentions with a big heart, like your mother Nut's, the goddess of the sky. The more clemency and sympathy you have given him, the crueler and more evil he has become.

ISIS I felt sorry for him. I responded to his hurtfulness with clemency. I was loyal to the principles of my mother, Nut, but it seems she was mistaken. I should have responded to his wickedness with wickedness.

MAAT Are you disclaiming the values of your mother? Are you renouncing your ethics and great ideals? Are you betraying yourself, Isis? Are you not seeing the dark road down which Seth is leading you? He wants you with him on this path. Since the time he opened his eyes to life, he has wanted you with him. Are you going to grant his wish now? Will Seth, the god of wickedness, prevail over Isis the goddess of integrity?

ISIS   It seems that evilness in this life is the more potent. Did the god Ra not triumph over my mother Nut?

MAAT   It is not Isis who is saying this!

ISIS   I will not feel sorry for him this time. I do not have any sympathy or mercy like Osiris. Osiris died and left honesty and justice for me. Justice is goodness for goodness, evilness for evilness, and butchery for butchery. He who starts first is the oppressor ... I will avenge the blood of Osiris from you, Seth. You will not evade my punishment, not from me, Isis, the goddess of clemency and wisdom. I will not forgive you the blood of Osiris. I will not be merciful with you like I used to be. Watch out for the merciful. Beware the wickedness of Isis. She is no longer a merciful goddess. She has turned into a devil ... the devil incarnate ...

MAAT   (*with sorrow*) O Nut, goddess of the sky! Have mercy on your daughter Isis. O you gracious goddess of the sky, or has the sky lost its graciousness since Ra has conquered it? Why were you defeated, goddess of the sky, and why did you leave the heaven bereft of forgiveness? Your defeat, O mother Nut, extends to us, to all women and their sons and daughters, headed by Isis.

Isis is silent. She bows her head to the ground exhausted by her anger. She sobs in a low voice and resists her tears.

ISIS   I do not want to cry. I do not want my outrage to dissolve and become tears evaporating like water in the air. I do not want to erase the anger with tears. I do not want to put out the fire in my heart. I will not walk the route of mercy and kindness. I will not forgive you, Seth, and no goodness will exist in the world after Osiris.

Isis dissolves into crying. She cries loudly.

MAAT   Cry, Isis! Cry! Your tears will cleanse your heart and your eyes. Tears clean the mind of the foolishness of anger. Cry, Isis, and fill the universe with tears for Osiris. Let the river overflow with tears. Let the sea overflow.

Isis abandons herself to crying. Then, after a few moments she dries her tears.

ISIS   What will the tears achieve? Crying does not help. Will Isis, the goddess of power and wisdom, transform into a widow lamenting her deceased husband? No! Let the tears dry in your eyes, Isis. I will never cry after today. I will transform the tears into burning fire. I will transform the grief into bright light. Evil will not conquer goodness. Seth will not triumph over Isis and Osiris. The god of kindness will live as long as I live. Osiris is not dead. Osiris lives. Isis resurrects him ... Wake Osiris! ... You are alive! ... You are alive in the heart of Isis!

A voice is heard in the distance saying "Isis ... Isis ... Isis."

ISIS   (*shaken*) Do you hear? Here is the voice returning ... I hear it ... yes, I hear it!

Isis stands up and listens to the voice.
The sound of her calling echoes like the wind calling ... "Isis."

ISIS   Do you hear? The voice of the peasant mother is clear now.

She is calling Isis from afar without appearing yet on the stage.

MAAT   Yes, I hear the voice. It is not the voice of Osiris. It is the voice of a woman calling.

ISIS   She is calling me. She must be a woman in distress.

MAAT   She is one of the peasants. I know these people. These women do not stop complaining and recounting their misery.

The peasant mother appears on stage. She looks terrified and abject. She is beseeching Isis.

THE PEASANT MOTHER O goddess of justice and mercy, daughter of Nut, goddess of the sky, there is no mercy left in the sky or on earth.

MAAT (*a bit harsh*) What has happened, woman? Speak.

ISIS (*compassionately*) Wait Maat ... Easy on her ...

THE PEASANT MOTHER My daughter, O goddess Isis ... My young daughter ... My only daughter, they grabbed her from me while I was selling in the market....

MAAT Who grabbed her?

THE PEASANT MOTHER I do not know who they were ...

MAAT Did you see any of them?

THE PEASANT MOTHER (*terrified*) No! I did not see anyone. I do not accuse anyone ...

(*she hesitates*) I saw a ghost ... I saw many ghosts ... One of the malevolent ghosts, not the beneficent ghosts, grabbed her. I cannot attest against any of the divine ... I wish my tongue would be severed if I said it ... I wish my tongue would be severed!

MAAT Do not distress yourself. I will make you a charm to bring back your daughter and ...

ISIS (*interrupting*) What charm, Maat, goddess of justice? Do you rely on magic?

MAAT Do we have anything but magic? I will blow into my pipes and beg the god Ra to give her back her daughter.

THE PEASANT MOTHER (*terrified*) No ... Almighty god Ra does not rob ... I wish my tongue would sever if I said that ... The wicked ghosts and evil doers are the ones who snatched my daughter ... O my young daughter ... Where are you now? ... I have not slept since they abducted you ...

The mother cries, exasperated.

Isis consoles and comforts her.

ISIS   Do not be sad, madam ... I will search for your daughter in the dens of the demons ... I will seek out your daughter and will not rest until she is back to you ... I know the monsters that took her ... They are the same devils that captured Osiris ... the god of goodness. They are the devils ...

THE PEASANT MOTHER   (*kisses Isis*) Thank you Isis, goddess of justice and mercy ...

Thank you, Isis

Daughter of Nut, goddess of the sky

Love of Osiris, god of kindness ...

Thank you Isis ... I will pray

Night and day, and will not relax until the goddess of the sky has

Mercy on me and my daughter has returned to me.

Isis   (*powerfully*) Your daughter will return to you ...

And Osiris will return ...

Kindness will return ... Yes

He will be back in spite of all the gods

Of wickedness!

SCENE FOUR

King Seth is on the throne speaking to the highest-ranking member of his cabinet, the army chief.

THE ARMY CHIEF   Everything is fine, my lord. Order reigns and everything is stable. All the icons of former male and female divinities have been removed. Only the pictures of the almighty god Ra, the god of the sky, and King Seth, the god of the earth, are left. All the representations of the departed Osiris have been replaced and no one will doubt his natural death, which occurred by the will of god Ra. We settled the rumor that he was killed ... and ...

SETH   (*interrupting*) And what about Isis?

The army chief continues as if he did not hear Seth's question.

THE ARMY CHIEF   We announced over the megaphones and with the hornpipes that the era of deprivation and degradation is gone, with no possibility of return, and the era of prosperity, security, and freedom has begun. There will not be any hungry or naked person and each peasant will have a house illuminated with the energy of the sun and the strength of almighty Ra, and ...

SETH   (*interrupts him*) And what about Isis?

THE ARMY CHIEF   (*continues his discourse*) The nation is calm, my lord. Security, prosperity, freedom, and order are everywhere. No one opens his mouth in complaint. And if someone does, we immediately take special measures to contain him to preserve order, serenity, peace and quiet, and ...

SETH   (*interrupts him*) And what about Isis?

THE ARMY CHIEF   (*continuing his discourse*) And for the sake of national unity, we have announced that the earth has only one god, King Seth, and that all the deities of the sky have been defeated and are dead, beginning with Nut. No one is left except Ra, who owns the sun, and no one shares with him the space around the earth. And ...

SETH   (*gets up irritated*) And what about Isis? Did you lose your hearing? Or, are you pretending deafness?

THE ARMY CHIEF   (*muttering*) What? About what? Yes, my lord ... I heard ... what about Isis? ... Yes, what about her? ... Nothing my lord ... nothing ... she does not have anything in the sky or earth ... even a house she does not own anymore. We confiscated it and placed it under guard. She lives in almost complete isolation. No one visits her. People are afraid of approaching her. We started some rumors about her. This war of rumors, my lord, results from our effective talent and will definitely destroy her. We initiated a big rumor claiming that she lost her mind because of her grief over the death of her husband, and that she imagines he is still alive, and that she is hysterical, hearing voices and seeing ghosts ... She hallucinates ... yes, has hallucinations ... hallucinations.

SETH (*angry*) You are hallucinating! She has her full reason and intelligence and I heard that she is leading a rebellious movement ...

THE ARMY CHIEF (*muttering*) A rebellious movement! I did not hear any of this my lord. They are rumors. Only rumors. The town is full of rumors.

SETH (*furiously*) They are not rumors. Isis is my sister and I know her. She has not lost her mind. I know her. She is my sister and the daughter of my mother, Nut, and my father, Geb. She inherited reason and intelligence from her mother ... and cunning ... the cunning of the gods ... She is cunning ... It is not good to underestimate her.

THE ARMY CHIEF Whatever she is, my lord, she is only one woman. No one is left with her. No one mentions her. All of them have forgotten about her and her image has disappeared from their memories ... As for you, my lord, your image is everywhere ... in every heart, worn on every chest, and posted on the walls. You have been supported by the army, police, megaphones, books, thinkers, the pipe players, and, above all, by almighty Ra, and ...

SETH (*interrupting*) I know all that. But when Isis decides to do something, nothing can stop her. She is solid like a rock ... she possesses extraordinary power ... I know her ...

THE ARMY CHIEF (*astonished*) Extraordinary power? I cannot understand ...

SETH   Yes, she has extraordinary power ... almost magical ... She is a witch.

THE ARMY CHIEF   (*astonished*) Do you believe in magic, my lord? We trick people with magic, ghosts, and the devils' phantoms ... I beg your pardon, my lord ... I do not think you ... pardon ...

SETH   I do not mean she is a witch. I mean she is strong and has a strong willpower that never bends. She will not cease until she gets what she wants and turns the people against me.

THE ARMY CHIEF   I know how to get rid of her, my lord. Leave her to me and do not think of her.

SETH   (*concerned*) No! Do not kill her! I do not want to assassinate her. She would become a martyr and her soul would roam the skies. Martyrs' souls are more powerful than their bodies. Her name would be more famous among people, her holiness would double, and they would worship her more and more. Look what happened to Osiris after we killed him. Do you think he died? Never! He lives maybe more than before. People get attached to fantasy. They fantasize that Isis has brought him back to life. People in our country are ignorant; they do not know right from wrong or truth from fantasy.

THE ARMY CHIEF   An ignorant public is better than an alert one, my lord. We have filled the heads of people with a lot of fantasies and none of the deities are left on the throne in the sky or on earth either.

SETH   But there is fantasy and there is fantasy! Why do you not conquer the ambition that creeps into the heads of people? Where is your control, you, my army chief? Where is the power of the army and the police? Where are the writers, thinkers, and the employees of the palace? How does such a dangerous illusion slip into the heads of people without an order from me?

THE ARMY CHIEF   We, my lord, are in control of everything. Nothing enters the minds of people except what we announce over the megaphones and with the horns and the sacred book of the god Ra.

SETH   I heard that some peasants are saying that Isis is capable of resurrecting Osiris. How has this illusion entered the mind of the people?

THE ARMY CHIEF   It has not entered, my lord.

SETH   (*angry*) It has entered their heads! I know it has! I am certain of this!

THE ARMY CHIEF   If it has entered their heads, my lord, then the matter is very dangerous. The ability to resurrect the dead means, of course, the ability to destroy the living. Whoever gives life can also take it. She competes with the god Ra in this power. Her existence has become dangerous, my lord, to the existence of Ra. And if her existence threatens the existence of Ra, then it threatens your existence too. And if her existence threatens the existence of the king, it threatens my existence too, the army chief, the second in line after the king. Consequently, she threatens all of us. We cannot keep silent in this matter. We must remove her from being. She must die!

SETH   Do you think she is afraid of dying? She knows that she will live forever in death and her soul will be pre-eminent in the sky. She will become like her mother, Nut, the goddess of the sky.

THE ARMY CHIEF   (*confused*) What should we do, my lord, with a woman who is not afraid of dying?!

(*He lifts his hands to the sky*) Save us, O god of the sky, Ra, from this dangerous woman. We have nothing left but to pray to almighty Ra.

SETH   (*humble*) Yes, let us pray to Ra ... The affairs of government and the state have prevented us from praying ...

THE ARMY CHIEF   Yes, my lord, we have forgotten to pray and we have neglected it. The god Ra might abandon us because we have refrained from revering him.

SETH   Let us pray now! Yes, now! Quickly. We still have time. Are you ready to pray?

THE ARMY CHIEF   Yes, I am ready.

The army chief stands behind Seth with his hands lifted to the sky. Seth stands still, looking at the horizon, towards the sun.

SETH   (*muttering*) O god ... O ... O ...

Seth does not know what to say as if he has forgotten the words of the prayer.

SETH   (*muttering*) Do you remember what we used to say when we would start to pray? My memory is burdened with the affairs of government and state and I forget ...

THE ARMY CHIEF   It seems I have forgotten the words too, my lord ... my brain is occupied with plans of war, which are many, without end. This does not leave any place in my brain for anything else ... Forgive us our sins, almighty god Ra, and grant us victory over the enemy of justice, Isis, the daughter of Nut.

SETH   (*furiously*) These requests come at the end of the prayer, not at the beginning. Also, we should pray without demanding an outcome; otherwise, our prayer will seem manipulative ...

THE ARMY CHIEF   (*regretting*) Yes, my lord ... we must pray without any requests ... O almighty god Ra, we are praying to you without any requests. I swear on my honor that this prayer is pure and we do not have any demands in this life or the next ... An honest prayer without exigency, except to satisfy you and obtain your permission to admire your face, lit up like the sun disc.

SETH   Yes, this is a just prayer that can be accepted by the almighty god Ra.

Seth and the army chief stand in humility ready to pray.

THE ARMY CHIEF   (*remembering*) But we forgot something important, my lord.

SETH   What is it?

THE ARMY CHIEF   That god Ra does not accept a prayer bare like this.

SETH   Bare? What do you mean?

THE ARMY CHIEF   I mean the bloodletting, my lord. The deities need the gore too. There is no prayer without slaughter and meat.

SETH   (*remembering*) Ah, you mean sacrifices?

THE ARMY CHIEF   Sacrifices, gore, slaughter, all the same ... There is nothing for free.

SETH   Let us slay a bull for him.

THE ARMY CHIEF   Almighty Ra does not accept a single bull anymore. That was before the vogue of higher prices and the weak production of bulls.

SETH   We have many bulls and calves too. We have also imported from abroad a new quantity of calves.

THE ARMY CHIEF   Almighty Ra does not eat imported meat because it is hefty with no taste.

SETH   Slay a calf of mine, which I have been raising on the farm of the palace.

THE ARMY CHIEF   One calf is not enough for the almighty god Ra.

SETH   Why?

THE ARMY CHIEF   Greed, my lord.

SETH   (*angry*) What did you say?

THE ARMY CHIEF   A slip of the tongue my lord. A slip ... I do not mean.

SETH   (*protesting*) How dare you mock the almighty god Ra in this way? Are you not aware of the punishment for disrespecting Ra?

THE ARMY CHIEF   (*apologizing*) Forgive me, almighty god! And forgive me, my lord! I did not mean any harm; I had good intentions. Praise to almighty Ra. All I meant was that it is becoming more expensive; all the prices are increasing, including those for sacrifices.

SETH   Slaughter two calves and almighty Ra will compensate you.

THE ARMY CHIEF   I will slay three calves with your permission, my lord; we have plenty.

SETH   (*furiously*) I said two. That means two! Why the third?

THE ARMY CHIEF   As a bribe, my lord.

SETH   (*enraged*) You are a licentious unbeliever. Are you bribing the deities too? Are you not satisfied with bribes on earth? Also, how do you expect a mighty god like Ra to accept a bribe?!

THE ARMY CHIEF   (*apologizing*) I do not mean a bribe as "bribe" my lord. Not almighty Ra. It is simply for taxes ... excise stamps. For transportation, tobacco, tea, and something like this. It is all paid according to the new law under the heading "taxes", my lord.

SETH   (*lifting his hands to the sky*) Three calves at one time, O mighty Ra? Have mercy on your sincere slave, Seth, who supported you in combat and struggles.

THE ARMY CHIEF   No one forgets that, my lord. Without you, mighty Ra would not have obtained the disc of sun or even one yard of the kingdom of the sky. Without you, my lord, Isis would have inherited the throne of the sky from her mother, Nut.

SETH   (*angry*) Shush! What are you saying?!

THE ARMY CHIEF   (*withdrawing*) Nothing, my lord. Nothing. Only foolishness. Foolishness, I have become feeble-minded, my lord, since I heard that Isis is leading a rebellion ... We are all in danger ...

SETH   Who told you she is leading a rebellion?

THE ARMY CHIEF   You, my lord.

SETH   (*confused*) Me?

THE ARMY CHIEF   Yes, my lord ... a few minutes ago ... You told me that she is leading a rebellious movement.

SETH   (*anxious*) Then the situation is very dangerous.

THE ARMY CHIEF   Very dangerous indeed, my lord. Even though I was convinced that she was stripped of her power and strength and would not be able to convince anyone.

SETH　Many of the peasants and the dispossessed believe in her.

THE ARMY CHIEF　Maybe the poor are convinced, my lord, but the poor do not count. They are simply a number. What is important is the class of elites, the descendants of the kings and gods. These are difficult to convince my lord, not less complicated than convincing the almighty god Ra. It is a battle, my lord, in which the one who owns the most calves wins. And we own the calves, but Isis has nothing ... Even the house she lives in, we stripped her of its ownership.

SETH　But she still has her mind. She does not stop circulating among people and pretending she can solve their problems. She claimed yesterday that she was capable of returning an abducted girl to her mother.

THE ARMY CHIEF　(*anxious*) An abducted girl! How did you know that, my lord?

SETH　My eyes! My private spies! Them, in addition to almighty Ra, who is with me at every move! He bestows his blessing on me ... unveils things for me ... and reveals to me secrets ... therefore I know everything ... Nothing is hidden from me in this life. I can hear the steps of the ants. The murmur of the wind cannot escape me. I am aware of every step that Isis takes on the ground. I know every movement of her hand and every beat of her heart. I know when her heart beats and for whom. I know who visits her. I know ... I know ...

Seth's voice indicates his pain and passion.
His voice weakens while repeating:

I know ... I know ...

He stays silent and absent-minded for a long time, then he exhales.

SETH　(*exhaling*) Yes, I know. I wish I did not know.

THE ARMY CHIEF	Knowledge is a kind gift from Ra.
SETH	(*dazed*) Knowledge is simultaneously good and bad. Ignorance is sometimes a blessing from the almighty god. If I had not been aware of Isis and what she does or what she may do, I would have lived more comfortably. I may even have forgotten her and erased her image from my mind. But she does not go away. She is with me night and day. She occupies my mind and chases away the sleep, calmness, and serenity. She is like a constant ghost on my chest at all times. I do not know how to get rid of her.
THE ARMY CHIEF	Getting rid of her is easy, my lord. The same way we got rid of Osiris.
SETH	She is not like Osiris. Osiris was plain and simple, to the level of stupidity. But Isis is malicious. It is impossible to affect her. She knows what she wants, and she does it with determination, without hesitation. Her will does not bend. Her mind does not sleep. I know her; she is the daughter of my mother and father. We were raised in the same house and slept in the same bed. I know her talents and her intelligence.
THE ARMY CHIEF	Her intelligence is known my lord. She was the goddess of reason and wisdom.
SETH	I have never seen a woman with such sanity.
THE ARMY CHIEF	Nor a man ... (*muttering an apology*) Pardon my lord ... a slip of the tongue ... I did not intend ... I did not mean ...
SETH	It was not a slip of the tongue. What came out is the truth. A painful reality; however, I know it is the reality. I admit I have never admired a woman or a man as I admire Isis. From the time I came to life, I have admired her. When she was a child, not only was she more intelligent than me in solving the problems of mathematics and geometry, but her pen was gliding on her notebook as she wrote poetry and music as well. She understood things before I

did. I used to become infuriated at my stupidity and myself, and the intensity of my madness drove me to break my pen or hers and rip up her notebook. She was kind and would easily forgive me. Therefore, I was left with nothing but admiration for her.

THE ARMY CHIEF   Admiration is a form of love, my lord.

SETH   Admiration is not void of love. It is, however, based more on hate. We do not admire someone unless he is superior to us. And because he is better than us, we envy and hate him. Deep inside, we want to elevate ourselves to him or bring him down to us so we can possess him.

THE ARMY CHIEF   You could have possessed her, my lord.

SETH   No! Impossible! I could not have possessed her no matter how hard I tried! She is a woman who cannot be possessed.

THE ARMY CHIEF   There are keys to each woman.

SETH   Isis's keys are with her. In her hand. She does not give them to anyone.

THE ARMY CHIEF   You have plenty of women, my lord. Isis is not the only woman on earth. There are many others.

SETH   But she is worth all the women on earth. Not only is she a woman or a female, she is reason itself. She inherited reason and wisdom from our mother, Nut, and I inherited from my father, Geb, the god of the earth, my body, greed, and the desire to possess. I was created from mud and earth and she was born of light, reason, and the sky. Yes, Isis is superior to me. She is better than Osiris and all my sisters and brothers too. This is a reason for loving and hating her too. I was torn between loving and hating her because I do not like anyone to be better than me. Nevertheless, I do not love anyone but those who are better than me. And as it is, it is I who am torn between loving and hating her. The more I love her, the more I hate myself. Why do I love her when she does not love me, when she is in love with another man, Osiris?

THE ARMY CHIEF We men, we always desire the woman who we cannot possess.

SETH (*continues as if he does not hear him*) Osiris was kind and stupid at the same time. Nonetheless, she preferred him to me.

THE ARMY CHIEF A woman prefers to love a stupid man to possess him and be free to do what she desires.

SETH (*continues as if he does not hear him*) His personality was weak. No manliness. Delicate. Shy like a virgin. Still, she loved him. I do not know how. A strange woman, like an enigma.

THE ARMY CHIEF All women are like that, my lord.

SETH No, not like this. She is different. You know ...

Seth approaches the army chief and puts his hand on his shoulder as if he is his best friend ...

SETH You know I used to peek at her at night. I saw them in bed together. He lolled in her arms like a baby in his mother's lap. She nourished him with her breast and nothing else.

THE ARMY CHIEF (*astonished*) Nothing?!

SETH (*dazed*) Yes, nothing! I used to see her body under the light of the moon like the thirsty earth in need of watering. Her bronze skin in the moonlight becomes an extraordinary color that fascinates the eyes. I saw the tiny blue veins under her fair complexion. I wanted to put my hand out and squeeze her with all my strength, squeeze her until her blood burst out.

He squeezes his fingers with all his force as if he is crushing something between them.

THE ARMY CHIEF (*excited*) Mercy, O goddess of the sky, Nut!

SETH (*suddenly alerted*) What did you say? I heard you calling "goddess Nut"?!

THE ARMY CHIEF (*withdrawing*) I beg you pardon, my lord ... a slip of the tongue ...

SETH   (*angry*) Have you forgotten that the sky has only one god, the almighty god Ra?

THE ARMY CHIEF   I have not forgotten, my lord, but your words excited me and perturbed my consciousness.

SETH   Do you mean that Nut is still alive in your profound thoughts?

THE ARMY CHIEF   My lord, I ejected her from my deepest thoughts too ... I expelled her and all women from my conscious and unconscious thoughts. I ousted all the feminine sex and I am grateful to the almighty Ra. However, your words, my lord, excited me ... They triggered in my unconscious spirit the desire to rape. I, my lord, do not comprehend any relationship with women except for rape. There is no other way to conquer women except by force. Have you not tried to rape her, my lord? Women adore being raped. I desired a young girl in the market. She was selling nearby her mother. I saw the calf of her leg beneath her robe and lost my mind. I abducted and raped her. Do you know what happened, my lord? Now she worships me and does not want to separate from me even though I asked her to go back to her mother. A woman, my lord, adores the man who rapes her.

SETH   This is the illusion that we, as men, believe.

THE ARMY CHIEF   It is not an illusion, my lord. It is the truth. This girl refuses to go back to her mother and prefers to stay with me.

SETH   To torture and seek revenge on you.

THE ARMY CHIEF   She confesses her love to me every day.

SETH   She hates you to the level of tricking you and persuading you that she loves you.

THE ARMY CHIEF   I am speaking from experience, my lord.

SETH   I am speaking from experience as well. Do you think I did not try? I tried to force her but ...

Seth remains silent for a long time as if the memory hurts him.

THE ARMY CHIEF   (*answers eagerly*) Did you have her?

SETH   (*with sorrow*) On the contrary, she had me.

THE ARMY CHIEF   This matter is too difficult for stupid people like me to fathom.

SETH   Yes, people like you cannot understand a woman like her. She is impossible for a man to rape.

THE ARMY CHIEF   Her muscles are that strong, my lord?

SETH   (*sarcastically*) It is not a matter of muscles! How can I explain it to you? My muscles are stronger than hers, but she is tougher than me. Do you understand?

THE ARMY CHIEF   (*confused*) No, my lord! What is the source of her strength?

SETH   I do not know, and this is the problem, or shall we call it the tragedy. The tragedy of my life! To be born into this life with a strong woman next to me. I do not know the source of her power. I love her because she is tougher than me. I can never attain her; on the contrary, she attains me.

THE ARMY CHIEF   (*astonished*) This I cannot understand at all, my lord.

SETH   You will not understand it! And I am not able to explain to you what happened when I tried to rape her by force.

THE ARMY CHIEF   (*very interested*) What happened, my lord?

Seth is silent and dazed, then, he speaks in a desperate voice.

SETH   (*desperate*) In her arms, I transformed from a dangerous wolf desiring to hold her, just before he swallows her, to a sweet lamb crying like a baby on her bosom, and asking for punishment or forgiveness.

THE ARMY CHIEF   O god of the sun, Ra! Bestow on us your strength!

Seth remains silent, dazed, and sad.

SETH   (*in a low voice*) It is so strange.

THE ARMY CHIEF   The strangest thing I have ever heard.

SETH   (*attentively*) No. The strangest is what happened after that.

THE ARMY CHIEF   Was there something after that?

SETH   Yes, I asked her to punish me and not to forgive me. At that moment, she could have sentenced me with death and I would have died with honor and manliness in her arms. But her heart was hard. She wanted to destroy the rest of my virility as a man and gave me what is worse than death.

THE ARMY CHIEF   Is there anything harsher than death?

SETH   Yes, pity. Ah, I cannot bear pity! Ah, I cannot bear her killing look. Ah, I cannot bear the soft tender hand, like poison. Pity. Pity. And nothing except pity!

Seth crumples down, sitting on his chair, exhausted, and tired.

THE ARMY CHIEF   You are tired, my lord, and need to rest. It is better that I leave you alone.

SETH   (*frightened*) No ... Do not leave me alone. Stay with me until you hear the rest of the story.

THE ARMY CHIEF   Is there still more, my lord?

SETH   Yes, the matter did not end at that. The last blow is still to come.

THE ARMY CHIEF   (*frightened*) She stabbed you with a dagger?

SETH   (*jokingly*) No. Not with a dagger, with something sharper than a dagger. It was possible to leave her and escape but I stayed in my place, incapable of budging, as if I were nailed to the ground. My arms, which hugged her like an iron loop, loosened and relaxed. She could have left me. But her heart was hard. She did not leave me. And around me her arms lifted to embrace me. Her heart was above my body, beating with pity. Not with love. Not with passion. Not with desire. Not with anything except pity. She was like a great compassionate deity, who bestows mercy on her weak humble slave.

THE ARMY CHIEF   Mercy, O god of the sun, Ra.

SETH   She disarmed me of the dearest of my possessions—my honor and my virility.

THE ARMY CHIEF   Take revenge on her, O mighty god, and you will get a fourth calf.

SETH	(*in sudden rage*) What did you say? A fourth calf?!
THE ARMY CHIEF	I hope the god Ra will pay her back with a wicked revenge.
SETH	The sacrifice will be limited to three calves only. Do you understand?
THE ARMY CHIEF	This is a new request from the god Ra, added to his previous wishes.
SETH	Make it for free ... (*clarifying*) What is the request?
THE ARMY CHIEF	The revenge on Isis, my lord. It is an additional request.
SETH	Do you know what it means for Ra to seek revenge on her?
THE ARMY CHIEF	Yes, my lord? The revenge of Ra is the vilest revenge.
SETH	(*furiously*) Did I not tell you I do not want her dead? I do not want anyone to touch her! This is an order! Do you hear?
THE ARMY CHIEF	Yes, my lord.
SETH	Leave Isis to me, both you and Ra. I know how to take revenge on her ... or at least I will try ... Yes, I will try ...
THE ARMY CHIEF	I have nothing to do but to pray to almighty god and ask him to watch over you, stand with you, and grant you victory over her.
SETH	(*exhausted*) I do not need your prayers, you infidel. Go now; I do not want to see your face or the face of any creature ... I need to rest ...
THE ARMY CHIEF	Yes, my lord, you need to rest ... May god Ra protect you.

The army chief leaves the stage.

SETH	(*yawning as if he is going to sleep and then talking to himself*) I need to rest ... I do not want to see anyone's face. I mean no one, including the god Ra.

He shuts his eyes and goes to sleep.

SCENE FIVE

On the shore of the Nile. It is dark. Isis is sitting on the side of the shore.

She seems tired and exhausted. With her is Maat. Isis looks at the Nile and from afar she notices the sail of a boat, which appears white like a light in the dark night. Isis wears a dusty robe like that of a poor peasant.

MAAT   You are beating your head against the wall, Isis. You are not tougher than your mother, Nut. You are not stronger than all the deities who were defeated and surrendered.

ISIS   (*tries to calm down*) I will not surrender ... The night will not prevail over the light. Tyranny and anxiety will not overcome justice and courage ... Desperation and death will not succeed over hope and life. Seth will not triumph over Isis and Osiris ... It will not happen!

MAAT   You are beating your head against the wall ... Nonetheless, the wall itself has ceased to exist. They have stripped you of everything, including the wall of your house where you were ...

ISIS   Vast is the homeland.

MAAT   They will not stop until they banish you from your country, just like they cast off the other contenders who stayed alive. We have no way out but to emigrate, Isis ... The world is vast ...

ISIS   No! I will not emigrate. This is my land, my country, the country of my mother, my father, my grandfathers, and my grandmothers. I was born here in the valley of the Nile and I will die here. I lived on this land and will be back to this land. Here is my house and my grave ... Here is my love and my heart ... Here are the memories of my childhood, the house of my mother and my parents ...

MAAT   They took the house and the people, including your relatives. They have left you too.

ISIS   I have a home in every heart. And I have relatives in every house.

A sail approaches. A sailor sings "The Song of the Sailor" softly far off in the distance, but the words and the melody are clear:

> You are safe and sound, safe and sound.
> We went and returned safe and sound
> You are safe and sound, O Isis
> You, the mother of sailors
> Love of the river Nile,
> You, goddess of the sail.

The eyes of Isis are fixed on the white sail while she listens to the voice of the sailor and the melody of the song.

ISIS   (*attentively*) Do you hear the voice?

The singing of the sailor echoes again with the melody and words.

MAAT   One of the sailors has returned safely and he is singing ...

ISIS   He sings to me ...

MAAT   He was out of the country and he does not know anything about the new regime and the new god.

ISIS   (*anticipating*) He is still singing for me.

MAAT   If someone hears him he will vanish and disappear behind the sun.

ISIS   (*ridiculing*) Behind the sun disc, Ra.

MAAT   We have to warn him.

ISIS   Yes, we must warn him. Do not tell him that I am Isis. I do not want him to see me like this. He must have imagined the goddess Isis as more beautiful than I am in my present state.

MAAT   I will not tell him.

The sailor pulls the rope of his boat and gets off on the

shore carrying in his hand a wrapped bundle. Maat walks towards him while Isis remains in her place, watching them from a distance.

MAAT   Welcome back safe and sound to the land of the Nile, my dear brother.

THE SAILOR   Greetings to you and to the land of my home, my dear sister.

MAAT   It seems you were away in the sea for a long time.

THE SAILOR   It was a hard long trip. I encountered a storm coming from the north and I would have sunk in the middle of the sea had I not called on Isis, the goddess of the sea. She saved me from dying. Before I go home I will visit her temple to thank her and give her this present from the Levant ... Syrian dates ...

He points at the bundle in his hand.

MAAT   (*in distress and desperation*) O dear brother, no temple to Isis is left. All her temples have been destroyed.

THE SAILOR   (*surprised*) How? Who destroyed them?

MAAT   King Seth destroyed her temples, killed her husband Osiris, and assumed power.

THE SAILOR   And Isis? Where is she? Did he kill her or is she still alive?

MAAT   She still lives. However, Seth chases her from one place to another, and no one knows her whereabouts.

THE SAILOR   O goddess of sky, Nut! Take vengeance on your appalling son Seth.

MAAT   Do not shout! If anyone hears you, your destiny would not be better than Osiris's. Terror has spread throughout the country: killings, abductions, and thefts. Whoever opens his mouth will end up in prison, dead, or deported out of the country.

THE SAILOR   May you have comfort in the next life, O god of goodness, Osiris ... You will be welcomed in paradise and you will live there harmoniously with the other deities and the immortals.

Isis rises and moves towards them in slow steps, in her long dusty robe.

THE SAILOR Who is this lady? (*He stares overwhelmed at the face of Isis.*) As if I have seen this face before ... And these eyes full of light ... Who is this lady?

MAAT She is one of the peasants ...

THE SAILOR (*staring at the face of Isis*) I have seen this face before ... and this halo of light ... Why is she so sad?

MAAT She lost her daughter in the market. She has searched for her night and day without finding a trace of her. The country knows no peace or security anymore ...

THE SAILOR (*addressing Isis*) Do not be sad, my lady, the goddess of the sky will compensate you for your daughter ... She will give you many sons and daughters ... The goddess of the sky, Nut, does not forget anyone ...

ISIS (*desperate*) Do you still remember the goddess of the sky, sailor?

THE SAILOR How can I forget her, my lady? Or how can I forget the deities of prosperity and mercy, Isis and Osiris? The god of wickedness can take my life but cannot remove kindness and love from my heart.

ISIS Good man, your words bring happiness and hope to my heart. Like you, I cannot forget the goddess of kindness, mercy, and justice. I cannot forget.

Isis resists crying, wipes away her tears while she whispers to herself.

ISIS Osiris, I cannot forget him ... He still lives in my heart ... Yes, he lives ... in my heart ... In my heart lives Osiris ...

She lets herself cry, she sobs deeply. The sailor consoles her.

THE SAILOR Take it easy, my lady ... Do not give yourself up to sadness ... We still have hope in life ...

ISIS Darkness has spread everywhere, good man, and discrimination has proliferated.

THE SAILOR   No matter how long the night is, the darkness must end, and dawn will emerge. Look there; my lady; a white light has appeared in the shadowiness.

A white glow like a beam of light appears in the darkness of the far distance.

ISIS   (*rises suddenly*) It is he! Or some of his people are spying on us in the night. Flee, good man. Escape with him, Maat. Take him away from here or they will kill him!

Maat clutches the sailor's hand and runs with him to the side.

The sailor hesitates in departing and looks back towards Isis.

THE SAILOR   And leave her alone? How can we abandon her? We must not desert her.

MAAT   She knows the way and she will come to us. Hurry! Hurry! No one must see you with her. It is very dangerous for you and her...

Maat and the sailor exit from the stage quickly. Isis remains alone. The beam of light approaches and illuminates her face. The light reveals her as confident and strong.

The voice of Seth is heard without appearing yet on stage.

SETH   Are you alone in the dark, Isis?

Isis does not answer. She is sitting proudly. Seth emerges wearing his shield and sword and a pair of bulky boots made of iron.

SETH   Are you alone?

ISIS   (*in a clear calm voice*) No! I am not alone.

SETH   Who was with you?

ISIS   Osiris ... was with me.

SETH   A man was with you a few moments ago. I heard him from afar. Who was he?

ISIS   It was Osiris.

SETH   Who was he, Isis? Who is the man you met in the darkness of night, away from the people's eyes?

He grabs her by her arm vigorously and violently. Isis angrily jerks away her arm from his hand wrathfully.

ISIS   Move your hand away ... Do not touch me ...

She pulls away and turns her back on him. Seth walks towards her slowly, trying to apologize.

SETH   I am sorry ... I did not mean to hurt you ... I cannot hurt you. You know that.

He stops talking for a second while standing behind her. He has sought to lift his arm and pat her on the shoulder or her back, then, hesitates. He does not touch her. He stands there silently.

Then, he says in a low affectionate voice:

SETH   Do you not know that, Isis? Do you not know that I am ...

Isis turns and confronts him with anger and interrupts him.

ISIS   I do not know and I do not want to know.

SETH   I beg you, Isis... Goddess of reason and wisdom, do not let your anger take away your sanity and rationality ... You are my sister, the daughter of my mother and father ... You are more than a sister ... and I cannot see you in this miserable state. (*He looks at her dusty robe*) And what is this robe?! Is it fitting for Isis to dress in this robe like a poor peasant? I cannot accept that ... I cannot!

ISIS   (*ridiculing*) Yes, Seth, my dear brother, the son of my mother and father. Your allies revolted against you and seized my house and my clothes without your knowledge. Why do you not arrest them and punish them, you great king?

SETH   What are you saying?! They impounded your house? They must be some of the extremists of my men. They think that these severe measures please me. They are more royalist than the royal king! Men like these are always among the entourage of the governors and the kings. A group of hypocrites ... I apologize for what they have done, and I will order them to return your house to you immediately. Not only the house, but also everything you ask for ...

(*He pauses for a moment*) Yes, I am ready to grant all your requests, Isis ... You know how important you are to me ... You are more valuable than anything in the universe ...

Isis moves away from him and does not answer. He continues somewhat enthusiastically.

SETH I am under your command Isis. Ask of me anything you desire.

ISIS I do not have any requests. I only appeal to my mother, Nut, goddess of the sky, and Osiris my husband, god of prosperity and kindness.

SETH Osiris has died and been buried.

ISIS Died? Who said he died? He was with me a few moments ago. Did you not hear his voice?

SETH (*angry*) It was not his voice, Isis. It was another man's!

ISIS (*surprised*) Another man's?! I do not know another man! I do not know any except Osiris, the kindest man.

SETH Are you in love with another man, Isis?

Isis is silent. She distractedly gazes at the horizon.

SETH Is there another man in your heart?

ISIS There is no one in my heart except the one good man.

SETH Who is it? What is his name?

ISIS Osiris.

SETH (*angry*) No! His name is not Osiris ... Do you think I will not know him? I will find him! And he will be punished! This time I will cut his body to pieces and each part will be dispersed to a different locale.

ISIS   Do you think you are capable of doing this?

SETH   Do you doubt my power? Do you doubt the strength of the king?

ISIS   (*ridiculing*) No, my dear brother Seth, I am not doubting your power ... I beg the pardon of the almighty god Ra, god of the sun, owner of the sky and the planets, who associates with no man or woman partner to share the sky with him.

SETH   Are you ridiculing the almighty god Ra? Do you not know the penalty for ridiculing almighty god?

ISIS   His penalty is death, like that of Osiris ... However, you are aware, Seth, that your sister is not afraid of death. If she were afraid she would have died a long time ago.

SETH   This time I will not intervene on your behalf with the almighty Ra. So many times I have reconciled him to you and asked him for mercy and to forgive your faults ... Without me, the god would have punished you relentlessly.

ISIS   (*ridiculing*) I will offer him a calf and prevent his wickedness. He prefers a calf from an unjust leader to the virtue of a just sovereign.

SETH   What are you saying? What did you say?

ISIS   Nothing. I remember since I was an infant what my mother Nut used to say: The virtue of a just ruler is better than the bull he sacrifices for her ... The almighty god Ra reversed the law of the sky after the defeat of Nut, and it is impossible, my dear brother Seth, for that power to be overturned without resetting the values and morality, including virtue.

SETH   There was no virtue during the era of your mother Nut. Women lived free and did as they pleased ... And the children took their mother's name and inherited her wealth. The father was merely recognized as such.

Even the almighty god Ra did not know anyone other than his mother.

ISIS   And what about the law of virtue in the era of the great King Seth?!

SETH   To execute a chaste woman if she is discovered at night with another man! Fidelity and faithfulness to the husband represent honor and virtue, and a woman can have only one husband.

ISIS   (*ridiculing*) And the man? His honor is to impregnate the women of the earth?!

SETH   If a woman has relations with another man besides her husband, the father would not be able to identify his children. And if the father doubts his children's paternity then how would he leave them his land and his throne?

ISIS   In this case, only those who own land and power need the law of virtue!

SETH   Of course! How would someone who is not my son inherit the throne after me? The sons of slaves do not inherit anything and it is not necessary for the father to know his sons. Also, slave women are not capable of being virtuous. The women of the bloodline of kings and divinities, like you, Isis, are capable of improving themselves through virtue.

ISIS   (*ridiculing*) Like adorning themselves with precious stones, golden bracelets, sapphires, and rubies.

SETH   Yes. How much more beautiful precious stones look on the breast of a chaste and faithful woman!

ISIS   And how more attractive the chest of a man may become when it is decorated with justice, virtue, and honor!

SETH   Yes, of course.

ISIS   Does the honor of a man differ from the honor of a woman? Does virtue differ from one person to another?

SETH   Yes ... No ... No ... No, of course not ... Honor is honor and virtue is virtue. However, if a man cheats on his wife, it will not affect the inheritance, because he knows his children. On the other hand, if a woman cheats on her husband, it is a crime.

ISIS   Virtue, then, is not *virtue* because it is not the same for all the people. It is an ambiguous regulation for enslavement. It liberates the masters and shackles the slaves.

SETH   The world is divided into masters and slaves. It is natural. Equality is against nature. Look at your fingers.

Seth holds the hand of Isis and opens it.

SETH   Look. The fingers of your hand are not the same.

He kept her hand in his hands and looks at her with love. He tries to charm her one more time.

SETH   (*tenderly*) I like the feel of your hand in my hand, Isis ... I miss feeling this hand in mine.

He kisses her hand and brings it close to his nose.

I miss this smell ... I miss your voice and eyes, even when you are angry. On the contrary, your madness and meanness excite me more ... This makes me love you more ... Isis ... my darling ... Why does your heart not sympathize with me? Why do we not get married? I swear to you, if you become my wife I will be faithful to you forever ... I only see your face in all women ... your eyes do not leave me ...

Isis removes her hand from his.

ISIS   I love someone else, Seth, and I do not love you.

SETH   Why do you not love me, Isis? Why do I love you and you do not love me? Why? Why?

His angry voice intensifies slowly while he repeats "Why? Why?"

ISIS   (*diverted*) I do not know why I do not love you, but I know that I love that kind man, Osiris. I only love Osiris.

SETH   (*soothing his anger*) Where did this second Osiris come from?

ISIS   (*diverted*) From the sky! A gift from the goddess of the sky! The goddess Nut felt sorry for me and gave life to Osiris, who was killed by his brother Seth for the sake of ruling.

SETH   I did not kill Osiris! I did not kill him! I swear by the almighty god Ra that I did not kill him. What should I do to make you believe me?!

ISIS   Swear by our mother the deity of the sky that you did not kill him.

SETH   (*hesitant*) I cannot swear by any other god except Ra.

ISIS   (*furiously*) And you abide only by the law of Ra?

SETH   Yes, the law of Ra is the best law and his holy book contains all virtues and high ideals. Have you read it?

ISIS   Of course I have read it. All he talks about is his holiness, his dominance, his superior power, his blazing anger, and his utmost revenge that he will inflict on whoever doubts the existence or does not obey him. I have not read one word on justice among people. He also divides people into masters and slaves. As for women, they have no place in the sky or on earth.

SETH   In all our history we have not known any doctrine which venerates women with the conviction we have for the almighty god Ra. What have women taken from ruling and the throne? What did my mother Nut, goddess of the sky, achieve? Her mind was preoccupied all night and day in philosophy, beliefs, politics, and the disputes of ruling. We did not see her much. I was deprived of motherly love when I was a child and my father was deprived from wifely care. What did my mother take from her life except fatigue, struggles, battles and wars? A woman is not born for such a rough, difficult life. A woman is delicate and frail. The body of a man is more robust.

ISIS If whoever is more robust must rule, why do mules not rule us? There is no doubt that a mule is physically stronger than you, Seth.

SETH A woman was not created to rule. She was created to become an affectionate mother and a gentle, quiet wife who waits for her husband with a tender smile, cheerful face, and a soft perfumed body ... Yes, this is the ideal wife ... Nothing disturbs her mind or heart except her husband ... I wish you were such a wife to me ... You would bear me the son who will inherit the reign after me. I want to put on your head the crown of femininity ... You will be the crowned queen of my house ... I will hold you in my arms every night ... I want you, Isis ... I want you to be my wife and lover ... You are a gentle beautiful woman who was not born to take part in the conflicts in the sky and the battles on the earth ... You were not born to wear these ragged clothes. You were born to wear silk and sleep in a bed, and leave the battles to me. I love you when you are this calm obedient female.

He pats her on the head and hair. He tries to embrace her but she pushes him away.

ISIS Obedient?! Do you know what it means to obey you? It means to ignore my reasoning and thoughts, to become a body without a mind, and to allow you to become my brain and my head. You do not want me as I am, and do not love me for me, a complete human being, a mind, body, and me. You want a flaccid female, a lazy relaxed body, which is decorated, perfumed, and adorned with jewelry, a stupid wife who waits for you, fills your stomach with food, and fulfills your desire of rape. She makes you a ruthless stubborn god. She pretends that she is stupid and cannot converse in important matters to satisfy your thirst for power and this disease of supremacy and godliness.

SETH I admit that your mind ...

ISIS   I will not deny my brain, Seth, even if you give me the throne of the sky and the earth! I will not transform myself from a human to a slave even if you and Ra order my death! Only now have I realized why I love Osiris and not you. With Osiris I felt I was a human being. He cherished me. Love is knowledge; value the knowledge of your lover. Osiris knew me. He knew my humanity and the most beautiful things in me: my mind and my heart.

SETH   And this second Osiris, what does he know about you?

ISIS   Everything.

SETH   Where did he come from?

ISIS   God's land is vast and kind people are everywhere.

SETH   This means you are living a new love story. Is this right?

ISIS   This is my own business ... I do not want you to interfere in my life. My life is my own.

SETH   Your life is not your own. As long as you live on earth, your life is not your own. Have you forgotten that I am the god of the earth and the one who sits on the throne and has the power?! I was able to finish you with one signal from my finger, but I gave you one, two, and three chances. Now, I am fed up, and you will not have another chance. As for this second Osiris, I will take care of him. Do not think I will not find him. Nothing on this earth is far from my hand.

ISIS   (*angry and defiant*) Don't threaten me! Your hand will not reach anything.

SETH   (*furious*) I will destroy him terribly ... and you Isis ... I will not grant you mercy after today ... I will not come to you after this ... I will expel your image from my imagination ... I will eject your love from my heart. I will leave in my heart only hate for you ... Yes, hate ... I hate you! Hate you! I do not want to see your face after today! I will not mediate between

you and Ra ... No, I will not intervene! May almighty
Ra curse you, Isis, daughter of Nut.

*Seth leaves the stage fuming and enraged. He beats the
ground with his metal boots and shield and his sword
screeches around him in a terrible hideous sound.*
Isis stands alone on the stage, quivering in anger.

ISIS May the goddess of the sky, Nut, curse you!

*The sailor appears beneath the darkness and with
him is Maat.*

ISIS (*surprised*) You are still here?

THE SAILOR We did not want to leave you alone ... We were hiding
behind this tree.

MAAT He almost leaped on Seth to kill him, but I prevented
him from saving your life and his.

THE SAILOR O goddess of justice and mercy, how has all this
happened to you? How can we stay silent about this
tyranny? I will not let it go! I will battle him with
the sword until he kills me or I kill him.

ISIS (*worried*) No! Do not duel with him! He will kill
you! He does not respect an honest duel ... He will
attack you from behind like he did with Osiris ...

THE SAILOR I heard him threatening you. He may kill you!

MAAT I heard him as well. This time he will not leave you
alone, Isis. It is better for you to hide in a faraway
place.

THE SAILOR I have a small house in a distant village on the shore
of Lake Manzela ... No one will know our where-
abouts.

MAAT Let us go there. The goddess of the sky sent you to
us at the last minute ... We did not have a house and
we did not know where to go. Come on, Isis, and
you, Osiris ...

*Isis is still sitting on the side of the shore. The sailor holds
her hand and kisses it with respect and humility:*

THE SAILOR You saved my life from drowning when I was in the middle of the sea and I brought a present for you from Syria.

He opens the bundle, which is still in his hand.

THE SAILOR   Syrian dates.

ISIS   I love Syrian dates ... and Syrian people ... I have among them relatives and acquaintances ...

THE SAILOR   They all think kindly of you and Osiris. And the sky goddess Nut, as well.

Isis notices a light emerging from the distance ... She rises quickly.

ISIS   He will return with his men. We must disappear fast.

MAAT   Do you know the way from here to the shores of Manzela?

THE SAILOR   I know it only by boat.

ISIS   Then let us take the boat, Osiris.

The sailor pulls on the rope to bring the boat closer to the shore. The three of them climb in the boat and make their way across the water.

The stage is completely empty. It is still dark and silent.

Suddenly the army chief and his soldiers appear with their lights and daggers. They are searching around the place. They do not find anyone. They look at the Nile. There is no trace of the boat, as if the river Nile has swallowed it. They leave quickly in quest of Isis and Osiris in some other place.

Complete darkness and silence on the stage.

ACT TWO

SCENE ONE

*In the large square in front of the house of Isis, Osiris,
and their son Horus in the village of Khibit on the shore
of Lake al-Manzela. The villagers, men and women
peasants, and children are singing and dancing.*
The group sings with music:
>Osiris
>Heart of Isis ...
>Osiris
>God of wealth ...
>God of love
>God of goodness
>Sing O valley of the Nile
>Osiris ... You are our love
>You are the heart of Isis.

*Isis sits with the infant Horus next to her. She is teach-
ing him to write with a pen. Osiris helps some male
peasants in starting their irrigator. Maat assists some
women in grinding the barley.*
*The children surround Isis and Osiris. Isis distributes
pencils and teaches the group and her son Horus how
to write. Maat offers the children pancakes made of
wheat flour.*
*The child Horus writes the letters and spells the words
while he eats his pancake.*

HORUS (*reads from his paper*) I love my mother ... I love my
father ...
And I love every kind person.

ANOTHER CHILD Love is virtue.

ANOTHER CHILD Justice is beauty.

ANOTHER CHILD Nature is virtue.

Some of the children repeat these words around Isis with melody and music.
Some children sing with Horus:

>Love is virtue
>Virtue is justice
>Justice is beauty
>Beauty is nature
>And Nature is virtue.

All the children participate in singing: (with dance and music):

>Beneath your hands, my mother, I knew the
> truth.
>I learned knowledge and wisdom. I knew virtue.
>You created me from nothing and planted
> the first seed.
>You planted the first tree in the land.
>You baked the first loaf of bread from wheat
> and barley.
>I wrote the first letter on paper.
>I knew the first melody of justice and mercy.
>Beneath your arms, my mother, I knew the truth.
>Righteousness is above power and justice
> is virtue.
>Beneath your hands my mother, I knew the truth.

An old man dressed in the outfit of a priest ... a rich silken robe ... a beard grows from his chin. He walks towards the children carrying his thick cane. The children stop singing.

THE PRIEST   What is this noise and clamor in front of the temple of the goddess Isis?

The priest notices Isis among the children ... He retreats a bit, humbling himself and almost kneeling in front of her ...

ISIS   Do not kneel, sir.

THE PRIEST   Holy goddess, I am your faithful worshipper ...

ISIS The faithful worshipper of Isis is not the one who beats the children and hates singing and music ...

THE PRIEST I take care of your sacred temple and receive the slaughtered animals and sacrifices ...

ISIS The faithful worshipper of Isis is not the one who receives the sacrifices ... He is not the one who dresses in sacred robes and grows his beard long from his chin. He is the one who tirelessly and eagerly searches for right, justice, and the profound meaning of things.

THE PRIEST I used to serve in the temple of your father, Geb, and used to accept sacrifices ... and it was prosperous ...

ISIS But Osiris and I do not accept sacrifices ...
People in this village are poor peasants who sell their eggs and cannot afford to eat them. They do not taste meat except on special occasions ... How do we ask them to offer us sacrifices, sir?

THE PRIEST And how do the deities and priests eat? We do not have a source of income except through the sacrifices.

ISIS We work with the people ... We plant and work to get our resources through our sweat ...

THE PRIEST (*surprised*) I have never in my life seen deities who sweat for their means of survival. What is the difference, then, between the deities and the people if everyone must work? It is the people who are supposed to work and suffer while the deities sit on thrones, where the sacrifices are brought to them without work or effort ...

ISIS This is the conviction of the god Ra, but the faith of Isis and Osiris is different. Our philosophy equalizes deities and humans, masters and slaves. There is no difference between one human and another, except through justice and mercy.

THE PRIEST (*annoyed*) And how do I eat if the people do not offer sacrifices in the temple?

ISIS   You eat by working like us and all those peasant men and women.

THE PRIEST   (*arrogantly*) But I do not belong to those people ... I am a priest ... and priests belong to the rank of masters, not slaves ...

OSIRIS   There are no masters and slaves in this village ... We are all humans. People are all equal. This is Isis, the daughter of the goddess Nut and the god Geb, and she works with us ... She married me, a poor sailor-man whose father and mother were peasants ...

THE PRIEST   You, the god Osiris, are the descendant of gods, my master!

OSIRIS   No... I am not a god and not of the lineage of deities and masters ... I am an offspring of slaves.

THE PRIEST   You are modest, a god of kindness and mercy ... You believe in justice and equality to the point that you make yourself equal to slaves ... No, O god of kindness and mercy, justice has boundaries. God Ra created masters and slaves, and this fact is mentioned in his holy book. If the masters and slaves become one, what will life and the universe turn out to be?

ISIS   It will be better.

THE PRIEST   May Ra forgive me.

ISIS   If you believe in the law of the god Ra, why do you stay with us?

THE PRIEST   I was born in this temple and still remember your blessed father in his goodness.

ISIS   And my mother? Do you not remember her in her goodness?

THE PRIEST   May god Ra have pity on your blessed mother Nut ... I do not want to talk about her unfavorably ... May Ra have mercy on her and forgive her sins ...

ISIS   Why do you not go to serve in the temples of the god Ra? There, you will have a lot of slaughtered animals and sacrifices ...

THE PRIEST   This is the temple where I was born, which holds the memories of my infancy. I was devoted to your father and wanted to serve in the temple, and die in it, as I was born in it. But if I do not receive any sacrifices or food from people, I will be inclined to leave ... Yes, I will be forced to leave.

The priest proceeds towards the wings but Osiris stops him.

OSIRIS   Do not leave, sir. Stay with us ... I will find for you an easy job compatible with your age, to live off.

THE PRIEST   Any job is an insult to me, master. We priests do not work and we are not slaves. I am used to sitting in the temple and having food brought to me, to my feet ... I do not work at all except for worshipping the deities and praying to them ... and this is a holy job respected by the gods, who appreciate it. It seems that the matter is no longer like that in this village ... Worship is not in vogue anymore and no one is venerating the deities ... I do not have a place here anymore ... I do not have a place except where worshipping is needed and the deities are sacred, and the priests have respect and reverence ...

ISIS   We are going to miss you after all these years ... Where will you go?

THE PRIEST   The land of god Ra is vast ...

The priest leaves the stage slowly.

The children return to singing around Isis and Osiris, and everyone goes back to work like they were. They sing and dance to the rhythm of the melody and the words while the other activities of planting, irrigating, grinding barley, and the flow of the stream continue ...

Osiris
Heart of Isis ...
God of love, god of goodness
You are alive in the heart of the Nile
In every green tree
In every drop of dew
In every breeze

In every infant's smile
In every song
You are alive, O Osiris
In the heart of the Nile and the heart of Isis.

SCENE TWO

The god Ra has called Seth to discuss a dangerous and urgent matter. Seth is standing wearing his dagger in front of the throne of Ra. Ra has not appeared yet. Seth is speaking to the high priest of Ra.

SETH   It must be for a serious matter that Ra has called for me so urgently.

THE HIGH PRIEST   Yes, it is very dangerous ... and the almighty god asked me to inform you about what has happened. He has ordered the death of a slave and you must execute the order.

SETH   What slave is he?

THE HIGH PRIEST   He is one of slaves of the almighty god Ra, who is assigned to serve and clean inside the harem of the god.

SETH   And what did this slave do?

THE HIGH PRIEST   The god caught him in bed with one of his women ... She was not just any one of them ... she was his favorite among all of them ... He chose her to be his wife, who bore him the heir to the throne ... He loved her and cared for her, and surrounded her with an impenetrable fence like a fortress ... She could not see anyone and no one could see her. The almighty god honored and supported her and relieved her of doing anything except eating and sleeping. Even her hands she did not have to wash after eating; it was the job of the slaves and the attendants. She was his favorite; therefore the best cuts of meat and the best sacrifices went to her, and almighty god granted all her demands.

SETH So what happened?

THE HIGH PRIEST The almighty god visited her from time to time after he finished from the matters of the sky, earth, and planets. He gave her all his love and attention and promised that only she would be the wife to bear him a son who would inherit the disc of the sun after him.

SETH And what happened?

THE HIGH PRIEST It was customary for the almighty god to visit her at night, but his passion stirred him yesterday in the middle of the day. Therefore, he left us during a hectic, busy time and went to her. However, he came back infuriated after only a few moments.

SETH What happened?

THE HIGH PRIEST He found her in bed with that black Ethiopian slave who was a servant in the palace.

SETH What a disaster! What a wanton woman!

THE HIGH PRIEST The almighty god has ordered the slave killed immediately and the matter concealed to protect the reputation of the harem.

SETH Did he order her killed too? Both of them must be killed immediately with this dagger.

THE HIGH PRIEST The almighty god ordered the killing of the slave only ...

SETH And her? The treacherous woman! Does she not deserve to be killed? She dishonored the almighty god. How can we let her live?

THE HIGH PRIEST I do not know. Perhaps he has a reason for that. She is pregnant and will deliver the son of the god and the heir to the throne in one month.

SETH Maybe he is not the son of the almighty god, but the son of that black Ethiopian slave!

THE HIGH PRIEST She swore to the almighty god that the slave did not touch her.

SETH   How did he not touch her when she was caught with him in bed?

THE HIGH PRIEST   She swore to the almighty god that she was asleep when she felt something beside her. She opened her eyes to see that black slave next to her. She wanted to scream but he shut her mouth with his hand and it was at this moment when the almighty god Ra entered ...

SETH   I do not trust any woman! Did the almighty god Ra believe her?

THE HIGH PRIEST   I do not know. But she swore to him that she was chaste and no one had touched her, except Ra himself, and that she is carrying his son only.

SETH   She is lying.

THE HIGH PRIEST   She could be lying, or she could be telling the truth. No one knows the truth except her.

SETH   She knows the truth, but how do we find out? How can Ra know that the fetus is his son and not the son of the Ethiopian slave?

THE HIGH PRIEST   We will know the truth after the birth. If the baby is black like the color of the Ethiopian, she is treacherous and must be killed with her son. If the baby has white skin and has the holy radiant features of his father, she is innocent and we will announce the birth of the heir to the throne.

SETH   How daunting it would be to have a black god inheriting the throne of the sky.

The god Ra enters with a halo of sunlight like a disc around him. He is followed by some of his entourage accompanying the Ethiopian slave shackled in chains. Ra ascends to his throne and sits.

RA   I order this black slave dead and ripped apart in front of me ... Now ...

SETH   (*drawing out his dagger*) At your command, almighty god Ra.

Seth hastens towards the slave to slit his neck but Ra stops him.

RA   Prior to killing him, I want you to castrate him. I want to see him before me, a body with no virility. Exactly like the body of a woman.

SETH   At your command, almighty god Ra.

The slave begs and implores, terrified and humiliated.

THE SLAVE   I swear by you, almighty god, that I am innocent ... I did not do anything ... I swear I did not touch her ... I was cleaning the room when she asked me to give her a glass of water ...

No one pays attention to the beseeching of the slave.

RA   Cut off from his body that piece of meat, which caused him to imagine that he was a man who could dare to look at one of the god's women. Remove it from his body with the knife to make him realize that he is merely a humiliated eunuch slave, who does not have a place among men, who is not a threat to the women of the slaves, let alone those of the gods!

Seth does what god Ra has ordered.

Some of the attendants hold the slave and spread his legs, and with a sword, Seth cuts off the testicles and the penis. The slave cries and moans in pain and fear.

RA   Now look at yourself, slave, are you a man? Are you able to touch a slave woman, let alone gaze higher, at one of the divine women of the god?!

SETH   Do you order his death, almighty god Ra?

RA   No, do not kill him. I want him to live in torture, shame, and degradation. I want him to stay a castrated slave, serving in the harem of the god, without me worrying about anything ...

The god laughs mockingly and guffaws raucously. The echoes of his voice resonate around the universe.

RA   Take him where the slaves and servants reside. Take

this weird mutilated creature ... Is he a female? Or, is he androgynous?

Ra laughs and guffaws raucously again.

Some of the attendants drag the slave on the floor bleeding and moaning in a low hushed voice.

THE HIGH PRIEST He has received his punishment, almighty god Ra.

SETH I wanted to kill him and drink his blood.

RA Death to a man is easier than castration ... it is a persuasive punishment. Also, when the rest of the slaves see him in the palace like that, they are going to be afraid, and none of them would think of repeating his deed.

SETH Would anyone of them dare to repeat that, almighty god?

RA Since it happened once, why not happen again? Those slaves are traitors by nature and you cannot trust them. They are the descendants of animals, dominated by their instincts, and they do not have any ideals, manners, or morality ... They are like women ...

SETH Yes, almighty god Ra. A woman is unfaithful by nature and she is never content with one man, even if he is the almighty god Ra.

RA The problem is that we cannot have sons who inherit the throne after us without women. If it were possible for a man to get pregnant and to give birth, we would have disposed of women completely.

THE HIGH PRIEST You are capable, almighty god, of making men able to get pregnant and give birth.

RA However, life without women becomes boring and it is easy to control them and force them to conform to our will and law. Besides, this is much less complicated than enabling men to become pregnant and give birth.

SETH The problem of the women, almighty god, is that

their desire for cheating is enormous and they cannot be satisfied with one man.

RA   We must constrain them by force ...

SETH   We must impose fidelity on her by the force of weapons.

THE HIGH PRIEST   And hang the treacherous woman ...

RA   I am afraid, then, we will have to condemn all women to hang like this ... Is there a better way, which does not wipe out all the female sex?

THE HIGH PRIEST   Not all women are dishonest, almighty god.

RA   Of course not, but how do you know the faithful ones from the unfaithful? They all cry innocently and swear that they are pure.

SETH   They are capable of lying and deceiving, almighty god.

RA   We must find a way to recognize the guilty from the innocent.

THE HIGH PRIEST   We could put a woman in the water of the Nile, almighty god. If she floats to the surface and the holy water brings her up, she is pure and innocent, and if the water let her sinks, she is guilty.

RA   Not a bad idea, but I fear that all the women would submerge.

THE HIGH PRIEST   In this case, excision is safer than restoration, almighty god.

RA   What do you mean by excision?

THE HIGH PRIEST   To deprive women from their excessive desire, because a woman, like a slave, is ruled by her desires. A woman's sexual desire is superior to her reason. We have to restrict this desire if a woman is to obey one man.

RA   And how do we do that?

THE HIGH PRIEST   By removing from her body the component of desire, almighty god, through excision.

RA   Do you want to castrate women like we castrated that slave?

THE HIGH PRIEST   Yes, almighty god. However, while castrating a slave prevents him from having children, circumcising a woman alters only her sexual desire, and retains her ability to have children.

SETH   A woman is born to bear children and nothing else.

RA   It is not a bad idea. However, I am afraid that the men's desire will vanish with the loss of women's desire.

THE HIGH PRIEST   No, almighty god ... The desire of men will stay as is, if not increase.

SETH   The ideal solution, almighty god, is to protect the body of a woman inside an iron chest with a key and call it a chastity belt. We can lock it when we go away and unlock it when we come back. This is the sole guarantee. No man will be able to open the chest in our absence.

THE HIGH PRIEST   And what if the key gets lost and another man, one of the slaves or the servants, finds it?

SETH   He will be killed or castrated immediately as we did with that slave.

THE HIGH PRIEST   In this case, prevention is better than restoration, almighty god.

RA   What do you mean by restoration?

THE HIGH PRIEST   To protect the woman from being desired by a slave, order the castration all the servants who enter the harem ...

RA   Good idea. We will kill two birds with one stone. We will protect the harem and guarantee that our sons are, in fact, our offspring. At the same time, we will reduce the procreation of the servants and, thereby, the number of sons descendant from the slaves.

Ra laughs happily and he screams saying

RA   I hereby order the castration of all the servants and slaves in our sacred palace and the circumcision of all the women and girls in our precious harem.

One of the guards enters and announces the appearance of a priest who wants a meeting with the god Ra. Ra orders him in. The priest (he is the same one who left the temple of Isis) enters slowly and when he approaches close to the god Ra, he kneels humbly.

RA   Who are you? And what do you want?

THE PRIEST   I come from a faraway village on the shore of al-Manzela called Khibit. ...

RA   And why did you leave your village? What happened?

THE PRIEST   O almighty god Ra, I do not want to betray the bread, salt, and meat I have eaten at the temple of the god Geb, but the circumstances have changed, and the people have blasphemed the gods, and none of them brings sacrifices or offerings.

RA   Is there anyone who has disobeyed my orders?

THE PRIEST   O almighty Ra, I do not want to betray Geb. I served in his temple for years and wanted to die there, where I was born, but there is no place left for me in that village. Also, no one comes to the temple to pray and bring me food ... They are all distracted from praying and worshipping by matters of living. They are busy with planting and working, and the separation between masters and slaves has been eliminated. The priests have lost their honor and are without sources of income as well ... I told the goddess Isis and her husband Osiris that I am a priest and it is not fitting for me to work as the slaves do but ...

RA   (*interrupting*) What did you say? The goddess Isis what? Are there other deities on earth besides you, Seth? And Osiris? Did he not die years ago?!

THE PRIEST   The goddess Isis brought him back to life. They live together and have conceived a son, Horus. I have told them that I am a priest and it is not right for priests to ...

RA   (*interrupting*) And they have conceived a son, Horus?! Are you aware of all this, Seth?

SETH   No, almighty god Ra. This news is bizarre and we do not know the degree of its validity ...

RA   Make sure of its authenticity. And if it is false, this man will die, for he has lied to us. And if it is accurate, I will order the killing of that fake god, Osiris, and his son, Horus. As for Isis, she is an adulteress who deserves to die, to be burned or stoned to death.

SETH   Your commands will all be obeyed, almighty god Ra ...

Seth walks towards the old priest.

SETH   And you, priest, come with me to show me the way to this village of Khibit on the shore of al-Manzela ... It must be a repulsive village, which deserves to be burnt!

Seth leaves accompanied by the old priest.
The god Ra and his high priest remain on the stage.

RA   Isis will not relax until she rouses the peasant men from the families of slaves against us ...

THE HIGH PRIEST   And the women as well, almighty god ... and if the groups of women and slaves join together, the masters and deities would have no place on the thrones of the sky and the earth ... Also, the priests will have no prestige, or even food, like that old priest.

RA   We have to nip this revolution in its bud.

THE HIGH PRIEST   Let us start, almighty god, by castrating the slaves and circumcising the women. He who does not know sexual desire, does not know the desire to control, and consequently becomes easier to dominate ...

RA   Yes, yes ... Let us begin.

The stage is completely dark.
Soon, a row of half-naked slaves appears. One of the priests wearing a doctor-like white coat and carrying a knife in his hand assumes the operation of castrating the slaves.
Complete darkness and silence. Only the painful and begging screams of the slaves are heard.
Then, a row of half-naked girls comes to the stage. The

*same doctor priest, with the knife in his hand, assumes
the operation of circumcising the girls.
Complete darkness and silence. Only the painful and
begging screams of the girls are heard.*

SCENE THREE

*In the big square next to the house of Isis and Osiris in
the village of Khibit, near the shore of al-Manzela. Isis,
Osiris, Horus, and Maat participate with the peasant
men and women in planting, watering, and building
bridges on the Nile.
They are all singing while they are collecting the white
cotton from the bushes.
The group sings with dancing and rhythm:*

> Light you give us, O, valley of the Nile
> Beauty be upon you, O, splendid you!
> Be happy, you girls of the Nile
> He is the god of prosperity and kindness
> Osiris, the heart of Isis
> Dance, you girls of the Nile ...

*The voice of a female peasant interrupts the festivity.
She is calling in horror.*

THE PEASANT WOMAN Isis! Isis!

*The peasant trembles from fear while telling Isis what
she observed.*

THE PEASANT WOMAN I saw them coming from afar like devils carrying
their daggers and swords.

ISIS Who are they?

THE PEASANT WOMAN I do not know. But I heard someone saying that they
are the soldiers of King Seth.

ISIS Seth?!

MAAT (*terrified*) Let us escape quickly ... Come with me,
Horus ... Let us hide away from their eyes quickly ...

And you, Isis and Osiris, escape ... disappear ... They will not spare anyone this time ...

Maat runs fast holding the hand of Horus.
The people run fast in horror.
Complete darkness and silence on stage.
Then, the noise of the soldiers, who come and go search-ing around, is heard.
The stage is lit.
Osiris appears, shackled in chains, surrounded by the soldiers and their chief.
King Seth enters, brandishing his dagger.

SETH   Have you not found Isis?

THE ARMY CHIEF   No, my lord ... We looked everywhere and saw no trace of her.

SETH   And who is this man?

THE ARMY CHIEF   They say it is Osiris, my lord.

Seth comes closer to him and looks at his face and hands ...

SETH   This face is not the face of Osiris ... This face is one from among the poor peasants ... His hands are rough and coarse like the hands of the servants and the slaves ... This man is not my brother, Osiris, the son of the god of earth, Geb, and he does not have any relation to the lineage of the deities. He is an offspring of slaves ...

SETH   (*speaking to Osiris*) Who are you, man?

OSIRIS   (*arrogantly*) I am Osiris, Isis's husband.

SETH   (*angry*) You are such a hypocrite, liar ...

OSIRIS   I do not lie. I do not have the habit of lying ...

SETH   If you are Osiris, the husband of Isis, then you must be my brother ... Are you my brother?

OSIRIS   No! I am not your brother! And I do not want to be.

SETH   (*talking to the army chief*) Did you hear what he said?

THE ARMY CHIEF   Yes, my lord ... He said he does not want to be ...

SETH   (*interrupting*) Do you see how this slave stands with his head up in front of me, King Seth?

THE ARMY CHIEF   Yes, my lord, his head is up, full of arrogance.

SETH   Decapitate his head immediately.

THE ARMY CHIEF   At your command my lord.

The army chief makes his way towards Osiris.

SETH   (*stops him*) Before you kill him, I want you to castrate him ... Cut off from his body that piece of meat, which caused him to imagine that he was a man who could dare to look at my sister and call himself her husband ... Remove it from his body with the knife, so he will realize that he is a castrated slave, from the lineage of slaves and not Osiris, the son of the god Geb, and the brother of King Seth ...

The army chief stands hesitant and incapable of executing this order.

SETH   Why do you not carry out my order immediately?

THE ARMY CHIEF   It is easier for me to decapitate his head my lord ... (*mumbling*) No matter how cruel I am, I cannot ...

SETH   You cannot?! What are you saying? Do you mean you are incapable of performing my order?

THE ARMY CHIEF   I beg your pardon my lord ... I am not incapable ... But (*hesitant*) decapitating the head is easier ... Let us cut off his head and get rid of him, my lord.

SETH   We will cut off his head and get rid of him, but before we do that I want to see him in front of me, a man with no virility, a male with no maleness ...

THE ARMY CHIEF   And what is left for a man if he loses his manhood?! Death is easier than castration ...

SETH   I do not want to grant him mercy ... I want him tortured before he dies ... I want him to feel traumatized from pain in the same part of his body where he felt ecstasy ... the ecstasy that is forbidden for slaves like him ... the rapture that is caused by looking at women from the lineage of deities and kings ...

The army chief still stands hesitant ...

THE ARMY CHIEF I am afraid my lord ... that I will not be able ... my hands are trembling ... my lord ...

SETH It seems that you are tired. You, come here ....

Seth points to one of the armed soldiers ... and orders him to castrate Osiris ... The soldier carries out the order of the king immediately. He cuts off the testicles of Osiris with his sword and throws them on the ground.

The army chief covers his eyes with his hands while he stands.

Osiris tolerates his pain without moaning and without bending his head. He remains standing.

SETH (*angry*) You still stand in front of me with your head up?! Decapitate this head immediately!

The soldier severs the head of Osiris with the sword ...

SETH Cut his body to pieces ... and spread his remains everywhere ... spread them around the earth and in the swamps. As for this small piece ...

Seth points with the tip of his dagger to the ground where the testicles of Osiris were thrown ...

SETH As for this small piece of meat that caused all these problems, throw it in the Nile, for the fish to eat!

Seth laughs, tossing his head back and guffaws, imitating the gestures of the god Ra.

SCENE FOUR

It is night. The stage is silent and dark. The wind is whistling.

Isis is dressed in mourning garments and next to her is her son, Horus, and Maat.

The light reveals the three sad, silent faces.

MAAT There is no hope as long as the god of malice is around.

Everything we build, he destroys, and for the second time he has killed Osiris, a kind person.

ISIS   He did not only kill him. He tore him to pieces, which he spread in the lakes and swamps ... and threw to the fish of the Nile! O goddess of the sky! I cannot imagine this cruelty!

HORUS   (*brandishing his dagger*) I learned to fight with the sword and I will avenge my father!

MAAT   You have the right, Horus.

ISIS   Right alone is not enough anymore ... You must have strength ...

MAAT   (*exhausted*) We do not have power anymore ... He threatened the people and they broke away from us ... Even Tut and Mastat went back to their holes and disappeared ... No one is left with us. Seth will not stop chasing us until we leave the countryside or die ...

ISIS   We are not leaving the country and we will not die ... We will resist until the last breath. And people will rally to us when they see that we are still resisting and have not surrendered.

MAAT   (*tired*) I do not have any breath left.

Maat collapses from exhaustion and sits on the ground.

ISIS   Let us rest for a while and then continue our route. We are not going to stop marching. We will not let Seth triumph. Seth's victory means the defeat of right, justice, kindness, and honor. It is a defeat for you and me and everyone who defends virtue. No, virtue is above power. We will not despair, Maat. We have a mission, and people who are driven by their missions do not cower.

HORUS   (*brandishing his sword*) I will kill Seth and rend him apart with this dagger!

MAAT   Yes, Horus. You must avenge the blood of your father ... But I am worried about you because the army, its power, weapons, and resources of the land support Seth ... He has everything, and we have nothing.

ISIS   We have righteousness!

MAAT   I am afraid ...

ISIS   And with us are the people ... People are strong when they come together.

HORUS   Only the sword can defeat the sword!

ISIS   The power of the people is stronger than the sword. The blade may triumph once, twice, or three times ... However, the power of the people is the only weapon that is going to prevail in the long run ...

HORUS   The blood of my father demands vengeance, and I will not calm down until I duel with Seth, and slay him ...

ISIS   O, Horus! My son ... I taught you wisdom ... If the battle is with swords or daggers, Seth will win. His only talent is in handling the dagger. As for us, we have reason, wisdom, logic, justice, and law.

MAAT   What law? He changes the law to suit himself.

ISIS   We are going to impose the law of justice on him ...

MAAT   And what is the law of justice?

ISIS   The law of justice is the law of the people ... the majority of the people ... We will assemble a public meeting and we will invite people ... a great number of people.

MAAT   The people are scared and none of them will come ...

ISIS   Why do we not try? We will not lose anything ... Let us start by calling Tut and Mastat.

MAAT   You call Tut ... He hesitates and does not like to participate in battles ... As for Mastat, he is ready to participate in any battle for justice.

ISIS   I will call Tut and convince him. He believes in justice and may join us if he feels that we have many people with us. Some people like Mastat are always ready and take their places in the forefront, the first lines, to fight for right. Some people like Tut prefer to wait a little while until some details of the tide of the battle become clear.

MAAT Mastat is true to his principles and his faith in justice. He does not care about winning or loosing ... But Tut is interested in the result ...

ISIS No one among the people is one hundred percent courageous ... people can divide themselves into strong warriors and weak combatants. And every person has some strong traits and other weak ones.

MAAT Yes ...

ISIS Do you know who asked to meet me yesterday?

MAAT Who?

ISIS The army chief.

MAAT What army?

ISIS The army of Seth.

MAAT O, goddess of the sky! I cannot believe it! Why does he want to meet you? It must be a trick ... Do not forget that Seth is a first class trickster.

ISIS No, it is not a trick ... I have information from some people who have assured me that it is not a trick. The army chief refused to carry out Seth's order and kill Osiris ...

MAAT (surprised) Refused? I cannot believe it. He is a cruel man, who knows nothing as much as he knows how to kill ...

ISIS He did not refuse to kill him but he refused to mutilate his body ...

The voice of Isis scratches from pain. She fights her tears ... Dries her eyes and almost sobs ...

ISIS He refused to slice ... refused to ...

MAAT (full of pain) Any human of flesh and blood would refuse ... Even a beast itself could not do such a bestial operation ...

ISIS It has become a sacred matter for Ra ... to castrate the male slaves ... and circumcise the girls ...

MAAT (holds her head) O, goddess of sky Nut! Have mercy on us!

ISIS   It is bestial! They failed to dominate the people with laws and the sacred book, so they have turned to castration and physical cruelty.

MAAT   And who performs these bestial operations?!

ISIS   The army chief failed to execute it, as well as his officers ... so the priests have become the ones who carry it out ... in addition to the sacred book, now each priest acquires a knife like a barber's razor.

MAAT   (*holds her head*) O, Nut, goddess of the sky, free us from this torture!

ISIS   Yesterday a messenger from the army chief arrived with a request to meet me ...

MAAT   We will not lose anything from this meeting ... But I am worried about you, Isis ... Maybe it is a trick ... Do not meet him yourself ... I will meet him instead ...

HORUS   I will come with you and bring my dagger with me.

MAAT   No, Horus ... I will go alone ... If he has anything to say, it must be a dangerous secret and I would be better off to go alone ...

ISIS   I will start assembling people ... We do not want to waste time ... Seth must be preparing to attack us once more ... and each minute is precious ...

The stage is darkened.

SCENE FIVE

Maat and the army chief are in a secret meeting. The stage is dark and it is nighttime. Only the faces of Maat and the army chief are revealed in the faint light.

THE ARMY CHIEF   Yes, Seth has become like a crazed beast. I think he has lost his mind.

MAAT   Absolute authority and unrestricted power make a ruler abusive; then he loses his mind.

THE ARMY CHIEF   I do not mean that he has lost his mind ... He is still thinking and planning to kill Horus, the son of Osiris ...

MAAT   Seth will not stop until he destroys Isis entirely.

THE ARMY CHIEF   He is a dangerous man ... the most dangerous man I have ever known. I have worked as his right hand ... and I know how he thinks. I have served him for many years and have carried out many missions for him.

MAAT   What makes you oppose him now?

THE ARMY CHIEF   I am not sure ... But I cannot continue with this cruelty ... Yes ... I have killed many people ... I was his partner in this brutality ... I was his sword and dagger ... But I decided to stop ... I do not know exactly why ... perhaps it was the last incident ... perhaps because I am older and tired and I want to do something good before I die ...

MAAT   Has he treated you badly? Has he fired you from his service?

THE ARMY CHIEF   No, on the contrary, he treats me extremely well. He bestows favors on me. However, deep inside me, I feel miserable. I have been miserable since I started working with him. I do not know why. Perhaps it is fear. Fear of the people I distressed. And fear of him, too. I have been afraid of his turning on me. He is an ambivalent man who does not keep a friend. His is always suspicious and does not trust anyone. He imagines that all the people around him are plotting against him and working secretly with Isis. I have sworn to him on the sacred book of Ra every day that I am devoted to him, but he does not believe that anyone is faithful to him, maybe because he is not faithful to anyone. He has imagined that all the people are like him. I have seen him getting rid of his assistants one by one. Sometimes, I think he is his own enemy.

MAAT   What a miserable man!

THE ARMY CHIEF   It is misery itself. I did not have one joyful day with

	him. Although I was getting richer and more powerful, I was not happy. Life in my eyes became joyless and meaningless, and I thought about dying.
MAAT	(*surprised*) You?
THE ARMY CHIEF	You may not believe me. I tried to kill myself more than once, but every time I would cower and back away. And finally, I have decided to join the troops of Isis. I told myself, if I must die, I would die supporting goodness instead of dying supporting cruelty. You must understand these feelings, Maat, you goddess of right and justice.
MAAT	Do you still remember that I was the goddess of right and justice?
THE ARMY CHIEF	Yes, and I still remember the goddess of the sky, Nut, in spite of everything. And I tell myself I must do something kind before I die to meet her in the other life ... Despite all the mistakes and cruelties, a human being is naturally inclined to kindness ...
MAAT	Yes, this is the philosophy of Isis ... However, the god Ra says the opposite in his holy book ...
THE ARMY CHIEF	He says that a human being is naturally bad and only Ra, and no one else, is goodness.
MAAT	The god Ra has seized everything for himself and deprived human beings of everything ...
THE ARMY CHIEF	Not every human being ... He divides people into masters and slaves ...
MAAT	The kings and rulers are the masters ... and the slaves are the poor, the workers, the peasants, and women ...
THE ARMY CHIEF	The poor do not have anything to offer the almighty god Ra, but the kings give him a lot ... Every day King Seth provides a minimum of three calves to almighty Ra. These donations cost the country an enormous amount of money and the budget cannot withstand it anymore ... However, the priests of Ra do not cease from demanding more because their numbers and their treasuries have been doubling ... They have

become a dangerous power, stronger than the army ... And they have acquired a dangerous weapon, more effective than swords and daggers ... It is the weapon of faith ... They communicate in the tongue of god and spread cruelty and fear ... And everyone who opposes this is an infidel, who deserves death ... Even the god Ra himself cannot control them ... They interpret his sacred book as they see fit, to scare people and collect money, and kill their opponents ... there is a great battle in the sky and no one knows its end ... and Ra is getting old and bedridden in his last days ... We do not know who the heir is after him ...

MAAT   Does he not have an heir? A son?

THE ARMY CHIEF   He has a son from one of his favorites ... among the women of the god ... but he is always doubting his paternity .... The priests say that he is not the son of the god ...

MAAT   Why?

THE ARMY CHIEF   He has a big nose ... and the nose of the god Ra is not big ... Also, the nose of Ra is lifted towards the disc of the sun ... but his son's nose is not curling upward ... it is almost compressed ... like the noses of the slaves ...

MAAT   Maybe the favorite of the god loved one of his slaves?

THE ARMY CHIEF   That is what King Seth believes. He imagines that all women are unfaithful by nature ... and every time a son is born, he kills him and the mother ... He does not trust any woman.

MAAT   Because he does not trust himself.

THE ARMY CHIEF   He ordered me to kill Horus and announce it over the megaphones and the horn pipes that Horus was not his brother's son and he was illegitimate.

MAAT   Horus is the son of Isis and the son of Osiris ...

THE ARMY CHIEF   Yes, and he is the only heir to the throne ... I believe this and many other people are with me ... That is why I have asked to meet Isis ...

MAAT   Why have you asked to meet Isis?

THE ARMY CHIEF   To tell her of my plan to get rid of Seth.

MAAT   Do you plan to get rid of him?

THE ARMY CHIEF   If Seth lives, he will definitely kill Horus ... And he may kill Isis too ... and kill us all ... His thirst for blood is endless.

MAAT   And what is your plan?

THE ARMY CHIEF   He commanded me to kill Horus, but I explained to him how difficult it would be to kill him without being exposed ... and that many people still believe in Isis and Horus ... Also, that the situation has changed in the country and it would not be easy to kill Horus without tribulations, like when we killed Osiris the first and second times ...

MAAT   Has he been convinced?

THE ARMY CHIEF   Yes, he knows everything and has his eyes and spies who recount what is occurring among the people.

MAAT   Many people are with us ...

THE ARMY CHIEF   I have convinced Seth that the best way to finish off Horus is to hold an honest duel with him in front of the people ...

MAAT   Seth will triumph over Horus ... Horus is still a young man.

THE ARMY CHIEF   Indeed, I know ... And I have prepared everything to kill Seth from the back ... The duel is only to persuade and convince him to stand in front of Horus ... Then, we will kill him without anyone noticing.

MAAT   It is a risk that may endanger the life of Horus.

THE ARMY CHIEF   I have arranged everything skillfully to guarantee the life of Horus, who will inherit the throne.

MAAT   Still, the duel is not a guaranteed risk.

THE ARMY CHIEF   Nothing is guaranteed in life.

MAAT   Isis does not believe in combat and victories with daggers and swords ... She wants Seth to be judged in a common court, in front of the people ...

THE ARMY CHIEF	What court? What law? Seth has changed the constitution and the law and made himself the god of the earth after the god of the sky, Ra. As for the judges, those who follow justice do not exist anymore ... Seth has bought off the judges with money and positions, just as he bought off the writers, thinkers, and pipe players ...
MAAT	Seth has not bought off all the people ... So many of them still believe in right and are willing to defend it in a just court.
THE ARMY CHIEF	No one can stand up to Seth or oppose him.
MAAT	Some people oppose him ... Have you not read what Tut and Mastat wrote?
THE ARMY CHIEF	Imaginary battles on paper, nothing else ... Some writers imagine they are heroes and, therefore, Seth has not harmed them. On the contrary, he has protected them when we were going to kill them. He used to tell us: "Let them write and critique because they are not harmful to us, but they are useful. They play the role of the opposition and convince people that I am an understanding ruler who encourages criticism and believes in freedom."
MAAT	What a deceiver!
THE ARMY CHIEF	He is a dangerous man ... shrewd ... and we cannot fight him without his using his own weapon ... cunning ...
MAAT	Isis will not accept deception ... I know her ... She is set on using the people's general court, and giving each side enough chance to accuse and defend ... Also, to leave the last judgment to the people ...
THE ARMY CHIEF	The court is still a dangerous adventure with no guaranteed results.
MAAT	Nothing in life is guaranteed.
THE ARMY CHIEF	Yes ...
MAAT	I am persuaded by the opinion of Isis, and many other people support her views too ... Do not forget she is the goddess of reason and wisdom ...

THE ARMY CHIEF   I do not forget ... And I do not forget her mother
Nut, goddess of the sky ... or Maat, goddess of right
and justice ...

MAAT   I am going to be the goddess of right and justice in the
people's court and with me other women and men,
judges whose conscience is still alive, not dead.

THE ARMY CHIEF   At your command, goddess of right of justice ... I
am your faithful slave ... What do you command?

MAAT   You must persuade King Seth to appear in court ...

THE ARMY CHIEF   I will try to convince him ... I do not know what he
will say, but I will try ... I promise you, I will try.

SCENE SIX

*The main square is transformed into a large court of
law, witnessed by numerous men and women peasants,
merchants, artisans, writers, and other people from a
variety of statuses in society. The poor and the slaves
are sitting on the ground.*

*On the right side of the square sits King Seth wearing
a dagger, surrounded by his notables; among them
are the army chief and some priests. Above the head of
Seth is an enlarged picture of the sun disc, illuminated
in the middle by letters made of light, reading: "the
almighty god, Ra."*

*On the left of the square sits Isis, surrounded by her
assistants, including Maat, Tut, Mastat, and Horus
with his dagger.*

King Seth begins by speaking in a loud voice.

SETH   In the name of the almighty god Ra, we start this
session ...

ISIS   (*protesting*) You have no right to speak Seth ... You
have no right to lead this trial ... You are one of the
accused, and the accused do not lead the court ...

Only a neutral person can head the court ... Is it not
so Maat, goddess of right and justice?

MAAT   Yes, we need a court leader from among the impartial
women and men who are judges ...

SETH   (*objecting*) I am the leader of the court by a decree
from the almighty god Ra.

ISIS   You cannot be the judge and the accused at the same
time. Also, the orders of Ra are not valid here. This is
the people's court and not all the attendees believe in
the god, Ra. The deities of the sky and their faiths are
numerous. We cannot force on this court of justice
one god or one religion ...

THE ARMY CHIEF   This is a logical view, my lord. The deities are numerous ... It is true we believe in the almighty god Ra,
but other people do not believe in him ...

SETH   (*astonished*) How can you claim this?

THE ARMY CHIEF   My lord, King Seth, this is a court of justice and
justice means that no god dominates the other gods,
except through justice.

SETH   (*angry*) The almighty Ra is right and there is no right
except him.

*One of the priests makes his way forward. He is a lei-
surely old man, advancing with dawdling steps. The
people quiet down and look at him.*

THE OLD PRIEST   People, we are now in the people's court of justice and
justice is that which is right above any power ... and
above any authority ... Any authority in the sky or
on earth ... Nothing will be our judge in this square
except logic, justice, reason, and allegation and proof.
Judgment at the end is yours ... yours, the people's.
The public is the possessor of true authority.

*The people clap for him in encouragement and con-
tentment ...*

ISIS   Why do we not elect this just person as leader of our
court?

The people clap in encouragement and agreement ...

ISIS   We do not need clapping ... Raise your hand if you elect this learned master as a leader for this court.

Most people put their hands up, except Seth and his assistants.

MAAT   The majority agrees ...

The old priest goes up to where he can lead the court ... In front of him there is a table and a gavel. He strikes the gavel and announces:

THE COURT LEADER   In the name of the people, we open this session ...

SETH   (*screams objecting*) I object ...

THE COURT LEADER   I did not permit you to speak, Seth!

The court comes to silence. Astonished, Seth refrains from talking.

THE COURT LEADER   And now, who wants to start?

SETH   (*screaming*) I want to start.

THE COURT LEADER   Does anyone object?

ISIS   No, let him start ...

THE COURT LEADER   Any objection?

THE CROWD   No.

SETH   I accuse this boy named Horus of theft and falsification. He claims he is my brother, Osiris's son, and he is *not* the legitimate son of Osiris. This son was born five years after the death of my brother Osiris. He was born in a village called Khibit, on the shore of a lake. So he falsely claims that he is the son of my brother Osiris in order to steal the throne.

Horus approaches, brandishing his dagger.

HORUS   I am the son of Osiris, and Osiris is my father, and my mother is Isis. Seth killed my father and ripped him to pieces and I will avenge my father ... You will not be rescued from death, Seth ... He who kills will be killed. This is justice!

Horus continues to approach Seth brandishing his dagger.

SETH   (*angry*) This lad is the son of forbidden adultery. I must rip him to pieces ...

Seth and Horus are going to duel with swords but the people prevent them. The court leader raps with his gavel and everything is quiet.
Some of Seth's supporters call out: Kill the adulteress ... Stone her to death!
The court leader strikes his gavel and everything is quiet again.

MAAT   Isis asks to speak, leader of the court.

Some of Seth's supporters call out: Kill her!

SETH   (*screaming*) She has ruined the honor of the family...

The court leader strikes his gavel and everything is quiet again.

ISIS   It is strange that King Seth talks about honor ... What honor are you talking about, you great king?! And where was that honor when you stabbed the woman who gave you life, your mother Nut? Where was that honor when you killed your brother Osiris to acquire the throne? Where was that honor when your supporters stole, embezzled, abducted, and raped? Where was this honor when you ordered the castration of male slaves and circumcision of girls? Where is that honor you speak of, my dear brother Seth? And who are you accusing of dishonor? Isis? Do you not know that the honor of Isis cannot be ruined, except by her own hand? My honor stems from me ... my deeds ... my love for justice ... my defense for right ... Honor is justice ... and justice is virtue ...

The people call enthusiastically, repeating: Honor is justice and justice is virtue.
The court leader strikes his gavel and everything is quiet again.

SETH   No one is arguing about the general meaning of honor, virtue, or justice but the central question, which I direct to Isis, is: Is Horus a legitimate son or an illegitimate son? This is the fundamental question!

ISIS   Horus is a legitimate son of mine ... I am his mother and I admit that he is my son.

The people shout enthusiastically: Horus is the son of Isis ... Horus is the son of Isis!

The court leader strikes his gavel and everything is quiet again.

SETH   Is he a legitimate son of his father Osiris? The son carries the name of the father and not the mother ... this is the law of the almighty god Ra.

MAAT   This court as we said earlier is free and neutral ... It does not concern the god Ra or any other deity in this session. Is this not true, court leader?

THE COURT LEADER   Yes. Seth, you cannot involve any of the deities in this court ...

SETH   I swear ...

MAAT   When he is unable to answer, he swears ...

SETH   I swear by the almighty god, Ra, that there is only one god in the sky and he is the god Ra.

The people laugh at the exchange.

MAAT   How can you swear by the god Ra that there is only one god, Ra?! You have to swear by another god to convince the people that your swearing is valid.

SETH   The god Ra is the one who triumphed over all the deities ... and he is the founder of this life and the next, and all eternity. He is the one who started the idea of oneness and consolidated the authority of the sky and the earth. He is the one who ordered that unification because diversity means division and separation ... Yes, this is the almighty god Ra, who has eliminated any form of diversity ...

MAAT   Except a multiplicity of wives, favorites, and the harem of the gods ...

The people laugh.
The court leader strikes his gavel and everything is quiet again.

ISIS   May I have your permission to speak, your honor?

THE COURT LEADER   Speak, Isis.

ISIS   The problem, your honor, is that we live in two different worlds: The world of gods and masters and the world of slaves, workers, and women ... The world of the grand deities with their desires, appetites, greed, laziness, and futility on the one hand, and the world of the poor and women with their minds, limbs, and their nights and days of exhausting work on the other. The problem, your honor, is that the world of the deities and the elite men wants to force on the world of the poor and women a cruel brand of slavery, under the name of the holy law of Ra. All people are born free. They are all equal and there is no difference between one human and another.

The people clap joyfully. Some of them call out: Vivá Isis, advocate of the poor and the slaves!
The court leader strikes his gavel and everything is quiet again.

ISIS   Then how does the god Ra contradict himself when he says that he gave life to people and molded their bodies in the most perfect way, and then he orders the removal of parts of their created bodies in the name of circumcision or castration?! And why does the law of castration and circumcision affect only slaves and women?

HORUS   (*screaming furiously*) Yes, this court must announce a decree to castrate King Seth and the god Ra in the same way they did to my father Osiris.

The people laugh and the court leader strikes his gavel.

MAAT Even the crudest calamity entices laughter. Is there anything crueler than this law, which imposes a double standard of morality? Which allows the masters all the rights, including the right to kill, oppress, and strip the slaves and women of all their rights, including the right to complain and file grievance.

SETH We did not forbid the right to complaint or grievance!

MAAT To whom should we complain?

SETH To the god Ra!

THE ARMY CHIEF Or to King Seth, the envoy of the god on earth ...

The people laugh. The court leader knocks with his gavel.
Seth stands fuming and then stabs the army chief in his chest with his dagger. The army chief falls, bleeding and moaning.

SETH (*furious*) Traitor! You who ate enough from my generosity ... And I conferred everything on you without limit ...

THE ARMY CHIEF (*moaning*) Only the god Ra bestowed on me without limit from his graciousness ...

The court leader stands up in anger.

THE COURT LEADER Seth has broken the law of this court, and killed the army chief with no justification ...

SETH He deserved to be killed.

THE COURT LEADER We did not sentence him. Why did you kill him without a verdict?

SETH I sentenced him to death.

THE COURT LEADER You do not have the right to sentence anyone to death.

THE PEOPLE (*crying out angrily*) Down with King Seth, a cruel judge!!!

HORUS   This was not the first one he killed. He killed many people, including my father Osiris ...

Horus approaches, brandishing his blade and starts dueling with Seth.

The court transforms into a duel between Seth and Horus ... The people encourage Horus. Seth is winning at the beginning and wounds Horus between his eyes ... However, Horus continues the duel and slashes Seth between his legs. Seth drops to the ground ... Horus removes the testicles of Seth with his sword ... Seth bleeds and moans from pain ... Seth begs Isis to forgive him and to spare him from the sword of Horus ... Horus lifts up his sword to remove the neck of Seth but Isis stops him ...

ISIS   Enough, Horus ... Enough ... Do not kill him ...

HORUS   He killed my father and I will not leave him till I kill him and cut him to pieces like he did to my father ...

ISIS   You are victorious, Horus ... You are the holder of the throne ...

The people call out: Vivá Horus!!

HORUS   He killed my father and I will not leave him till I kill him and cut him to pieces like he did to my father,

ISIS   You are stronger and the stronger is he who forgives ... Forgive when you are capable ... Is this not one of the principles of Isis and Osiris?!

The people call out enthusiastically: Vivá Isis, the goddess of mercy!!!

Then the people surround Isis and Horus and sing together with melodious music and dance.

> Isis, goddess of mercy
> Goddess of reason and wisdom
> Osiris, god of goodness
> God of love and kindness
> Horus, O, Horus
> The son of Isis

And Osiris ...
Horus, our love
Horus, our king
Sing, O valley of the Nile
Horus
The son of Isis.

Author's Note

Many writers have written about Isis, the ancient Egyptian goddess, but no one credits her as a teacher, thinker, and inventor of agriculture, bread maker, and writer, nor do they portray her accurately as a figure who had a philosophy, values, and religion. Her cult spread her teachings in Egypt and in Europe and survived all kinds of opposition until the sixth century.

Many writers have ignored this truth about Isis and considered her merely the wife of Osiris. They have formed a mundane image of her based on her loyalty to her husband and her role as a mother. An example of such a portrayal is her role in the play *Isis*, written by Tawfiq al-Hakim, in which he limits the character of Isis to that of a woman who lost her husband and is determined to bring him back. Al-Hakim compares Isis to Sheherezade and Penelope, who also supported their husbands. He transforms Isis into a silent figure unable to participate in the debates among philosophers and writers, and ready to forfeit her values for the sake of her husband. He did not recognize Isis as the goddess of wisdom, reason, and determination who was also known for her justice and goodness. Instead, as a male writer who believes in the concept of honor set out in paternal codes and connected to women's chastity, he forces Isis to defend herself against the vicious accusations of her cruel brother, Seth. The brother accuses his sister, who has refused to marry him, of infidelity, believing that Horus is not the son of her husband, Osiris. Therefore, al-Hakim stresses the relationship between honor and women, and ties women's existence to biological functions.

Tales from Egyptian history recount that Isis's role was not limited to fertility and reproduction. She, like her mother, Nut, goddess of the sky, and her sister, Maat, goddess of justice, shared high sacred positions with male gods. In fact, according to ancient history, the throne passed down through the female and not the male line. It was only later that patriarchal religions diminished the role of woman and associated her with sin. Isis also recreated Osiris after he was cut into pieces by Seth, and she was able to reconstruct and rebuild what he had destroyed. She was the maker and the creator of Osiris, the good man, and Horus, the son to whom she taught compassion, reason, and wisdom. The ancient myths and tales are interpreted differently by each writer according to the beliefs and views of each of them. Therefore, a writer has the right to explain these narratives in light of the proven facts.

Translated and summarized by Rihab Kassatly Bagnole

GOD RESIGNS
AT THE SUMMIT MEETING

A One-Act Play

Introduction

Nawal El Saadawi wrote *God Resigns at the Summit Meeting* after many years of study and critique of individual aspects of Islam, Christianity, and Judaism. The play is a reasoned (and at times extremely funny) investigation into the roots, mythologies, and absurdities of these religions. El Saadawi has argued against distortions of Islam that allow patriarchal oppression of women throughout the body of her writing and against the capitalism of Christian, Jewish, and Muslim religions that connive to suppress ordinary people. In her novel, *Love in the Kingdom of Oil*, the people are forced to mine oil at the same time as it pollutes every aspect of their lives. Both in that text and most notably in her play, *Isis*, she examines how old religions that celebrated women were subverted by developing patriarchal forces that culminated in the creation of the Abrahamic monotheistic male god. Now she takes both God and his prime representatives, Moses, Abraham, Christ, and Muhammad, to task at a summit meeting where God has finally agreed to meet his people all together to hear their grievances. *God Resigns at the Summit Meeting* is an epic platonic debate in which Nawal El Saadawi finally brings together all her thinking about monotheistic religion as an oppressive construct.

I had known a little of Nawal El Saadawi's work in the area of women's rights since I was a student in the 1980s, but it was only much more recently, when researching African women's writing and theater for a course I am teaching, that I began to study her work in depth. I am an Africanist and a theater practitioner, and Anglophone Africanists tend to prioritize sub-Saharan Africa, often seeing North Africa as culturally, linguistically, and religiously separated from the rest of the continent in ways that do not really hold up to academic scrutiny. But in the 1990s when I was working predominantly on theater in the Sahelian nations of Ethiopia, Eritrea, and the Sudan I began to want to know more about North African women's drama. The problem was that much of it is available only in Arabic—which I don't speak—or a little in French—which I speak very badly. I was, therefore, delighted to find a translation of Nawal El Saadawi's play about her time in prison, *Twelve Women in a Cell*, in the volume *Plays by Mediterranean Women* (1994). Then in 2002, when I was editing a book called *African Theatre: Women*, one of our contributors, Dina Amin, sent me a fascinating article about the play *Isis*, a work which was at the time frustratingly not available to those of us with linguistic shortcomings such as my own. I did, however, start to read some of the novels and polemic that are available in English, and when I developed an undergraduate course at the University of Leeds called Four Women Write Africa in 2005, El Saadawi was immediately enormously popular with my students as a representative of North Africa and writers of Islamic heritage.

In the autumn of 2007 I finally met a woman whose work I found immensely stimulating, moving, and didactic in the best sense of providing me with a rich seam of learning and whose life of dedicated activism one can do nothing but honor. El Saadawi was on a book tour promoting the reissue of some of her most famous novels and she kindly agreed to speak as a guest of the Leeds University Centre of African Studies. She was undertaking an exhausting tour of the world, largely because she couldn't return to Egypt due to the—at the time of writing still unresolved—furor provoked by *God Resigns at the Summit Meeting* that had led to legal proceedings being instituted against her for apostasy. Egypt's loss was Leeds's gain as several hundred students from many disciplines gathered for a hugely stimulating and entertaining public conversation that covered topics as varied as politics, medicine, women, patriarchy, and sex, on all of which topics El Saadawi was knowledgeable, provocative, and witty. It was on this occasion that she kindly agreed to send me the manuscripts of English translations of *Isis* and *God Resigns at the Summit Meeting* and asked me to write this introduction to the first English language publication of the play.

God Resigns at the Summit Meeting begins by invoking the founders of Islam, Christianity, and Judaism as they come together, by chance, in the desert to lament the failure of God's promises to his people. Moses wants to know why the Promised Land still doesn't have the extensive boundaries promised by the Lord. Christ questions why his father betrayed him on the cross and downplayed the role of his mother who remained with him to the bitter end, while Muhammad wonders why God has allowed corrupt Islamic leaders to prosper and Christians and Jews to become more economically powerful than the faithful. All want to know why God never speaks back to them however much they pray to him. So far, so Abrahamic. But Satan, who says he wants to resign his job because all he receives for his work is curses, then joins the complainants. Finally, two women appear. Eve is perhaps unsurprising, but a young girl no one recognizes accompanies her. Satan asks who she is and she tells him she is Bint Allah—the daughter of Allah. In a delightfully playful moment, Satan then enquires who gave her this beautiful name and Bint Allah replies, "The authoress." The idea of Allah having a daughter is both transgressive and teasing—and a beautiful counterpart to Christ as the Son of God.

This group, along with a crowd of ordinary people, then demands entry to heaven to speak with God. God's messenger, Radwan, had intended to let in only the great prophets, and then only after suitable offerings were given, but the people rush the doors and so we find ourselves before the throne of the deity.

Now El Saadawi allows her characters to speak their complaints to their Lord, and many of these feature his injustice—particularly his injustice to women. Why, asks Abraham, did God tell him to throw his second wife Hagar and her child Ishmael into the desert just to satisfy the jealousy of his first wife, on whose instructions he had been acting when he married Hagar? Bint Allah is particularly hot on the issue of historical ill-treatment of women. Why, she asks, did God order "the children of Israel to kill the women prisoners among the people of Canaan and Palestine who were not virgins, and at the same time hand over all the virgins to the soldiers so that they could rape them?" Gradually God is exposed as a bully, demanding sacrifices, even of boys' foreskins as "a symbol of obedience and submission to me, a duty to be fulfilled by all my slaves," but also as a man who has no answers to his complainants.

Two more iconic women, Mary and Isis, join Eve and Bint Allah and more and more unanswerable but logical complaints are brought against God. Bint Allah wants to know why God has allowed millions of people of the Book to fight each other in his name. And increasingly, God is asked why he has allowed his Books to be so opaque, so open to contradictory interpretations that allow it to be used for evil rather than good. More and more the people suggest that a new prophet might be needed—and this time she may be female.

The final significant female character El Saadawi introduces is the Sufi mystic, Rabia al-Adaweya, who advocates unity with Allah through love and destruction of the ego. The other women honor Rabia but Isis tells her that the name *Allah* is in fact adopted from an ancient female goddess al-Lat, while Bint Allah argues that it is important to unite body, mind, and spirit, not separate them as God and men do, fearing women's bodies and creative richness.

It is impossible here to discuss the entire social, political, spiritual, and religious ideas El Saadawi raises through her intensely reasonable and reasoning characters. Finally, they penetrate God's carapace of arrogance. In a long speech God repents his sexism, racism, and favoritism towards the rich and powerful and, above all, his long history of self-worship. He confesses that he stole most of his ideas—and certainly those about male supremacy and the division of mind and body—from older gods and that these ideas are wrong. He also says that there cannot be love where God rules through fear and that he is no more than "an idea, in the imagination." God is lonely and wishes to resign and to live as a human being.

One might think this would be the end of the play, but El Saadawi offers a final meta-theatrical twist to her tale. The stage goes dark and then the lights come up on Bint Allah, alone. We hear knocking on a door before it is broken down and the police enter carrying a book. The book is the play, and Bint Allah now merges with Nawal El Saadawi when she acknowledges that she is its author. The Chief of Police orders Bint Allah to be manacled, to which, in a riposte to the idea of God as being only in the imagination, Bint Allah says "it's only a play: something imagined" and the Chief of Police rejoins, "Do you want it to be real also?"

Left in chains, Bint Allah sings of a father who kills his mother and denies his daughter, recognizing only sons as his descendants, before in a last image she is joined by a large group of women, youths and children along with the prophets from the play, who simultaneously join together to break down her door and liberate her from her prison cell.

It would be impossible to summarize such a great portmanteau of a play. El Saadawi has poured into it her research about history and mythology, her research into the Qur'an, her medical knowledge, her political views, and her understanding of the ages-old oppression of women and children. In all these areas she interrogates God, asking why, if he embodies justice and love, he has so often and so repeatedly failed to offer these to his people. However, she then goes further. She starts to interrogate the origins of our concept of God as delivered in the Qur'an, the Bible, and the Torah, and argues, with examples, that our ideas of the divinity have been appropriated from a range of earlier gods and then manipulated to serve ideas of hierarchy and patriarchy that have culminated in this picture of an irascible old man up in the sky.

Finally she gives us her most challenging vision, that God is a cultural construct of the imagination. He is an idea, presented in a book in just the same way that any other work of fiction may be produced. Her book, this play, is seen as simply another imaginative idea, but the fear of the Chief of Police is that published ideas, such as these, may take on a life of their own. His final line is: "Do you want it [Bint Allah's book which is this play] to be real?" Of course El Saadawi and Bint Allah do want the book to be real, both in the sense that the play is seen and read, and in that its ideas about God might start to supersede those of the religious books.

Given this scene of confrontation it is deeply ironic that El Saadawi is facing court action over her play. The male state protection of the status quo that she predicts is being enacted as I write and if the playwright were not abroad she might be in the very cell Bint Allah inhabits. The truth of her work is arguably being demonstrated by the fact that the reaction of the authorities to her play is precisely the same as in *God Resigns at the Summit Meeting*. Imagination and reality, truth and ideas, are coming together in the struggle for control of, or liberation from, coercive concepts of the divine.

I am, of course, at a disadvantage in reading this text only in an English translation, though the writer gives helpful explanations of concepts, such as the name Bint Allah, so that non-Arabic readers may understand their significance. I am also, however, reading a form of religious translation. As a reader of Christian background I necessarily read a play of Islamic heritage differently than a Muslim would. I am struck by how the Islamic concept of justice echoes through the play in constant questions about why God is unjust. It is not that the concept which is more central to a Christian ideal of God, love, is missing, but that it does not take center stage, and given that this play is directed at Christians, Muslims, and Jews I wonder what similar strangeness a Jewish reader might find.

Then, of course, reading a play on a page, instead of seeing it per-formed, is always an act of translation. It is deeply regrettable that El

Saadawi's plays continue to be available only as published scripts rather than as performed theater. I find resonance in her work with the great Kenyan dissident playwright and novelist, Ngugi wa Thiong'o, whose plays, such as *The Trial of Dedan Kimathi* and *I Will Marry When I Want*, have a similarly epic scope, invoking world history, the masses of the oppressed, and anti-capitalist, anti-Christian, and anti-sexist rhetoric.

I hope that the English language translation of *God Resigns at the Summit Meeting* will allow the work entrance into the public sphere since the Arabic publisher had to withdraw his copies from the market in Egypt. I also hope that the text attracts proper critical attention, and promotes real debate about the range of ideas that El Saadawi raises. And finally, I would love to see a production of one of her plays, so that we can really see how the passion, polemic, and the comedy come alive on stage.

Jane Plastow

Cast

Moses, Prophet of the Jews*

He is dressed in the garments of a Jewish rabbi. He is short and thin with small deep-set eyes. He is about fifty years old. His complexion is dark like the ancient Egyptians and his pronunciation tends to be nasal. He wears black leather sandals with thick heels and occasionally stamps with them on the ground when angry. He rarely smiles.

Jesus Christ, the Messiah of the Christians*

He is considered to be the Son of God. As is customary, he is a handsome youth with long brown hair, a silky long beard, and a fair complexion. His garments drop wide around his upright body, his feet are bare, and he walks with long, quick, unhesitating strides. His voice has a powerful, youthful ring and resounds clearly.

Muhammad, Prophet of the Muslims*

He is clothed in Saudi garments. He is tall, has broad shoulders, and a handsome face. He walks with a measured stride, treading firmly on the ground. He wears open leather slippers like the Arab Bedouins, has a luxurious beard, and speaks in dignified quiet tones, smiling frequently as though confident in the effect his words will have.

Abraham, the Father of all Prophets*

He is an old man of seventy, wearing the clothes of a wandering Bedouin, tall, with a body hardened by the desert into skin and bone. His tone of voice is irritable, sharp with exhaustion.

Radwan, Keeper of the Gates of Paradise*

Still in his forties, he resembles the Prophet Abraham, shows the characteristics of someone who is the secretary of a very important person since he alone lets people into the presence of Allah (God). He is a frightened lamb in the presence of his Master, but becomes an angry lion with the people waiting at the gates to be let in.

Eve*

She is a young slender woman with attractive features and a graceful walk. She wears a long ample garment; her hair is black with thick tresses coiled around her head in two braids. She is barefoot. Her voice is sweet and strong.

*The Virgin Mary**
Resembles paintings of her in churches.

*The daughter of Allah (God)**
She is a girl, twenty-eight years old, who resembles Eve and looks as though she could be her daughter. But her hair is cut short and on her feet she wears a pair of dancing shoes. She steps lightly over the ground and sometimes dances. Her dress is short above her knees.

*Eblis or Satan**
A young man of thirty, handsome, and rather attractive in his ways, his complexion slightly tanned and his hair thick and black. He wears a colored shirt and baggy trousers soft, flat, leather shoes and walks with an agile step. His voice is melodious and he sometimes sings to the accompaniment of an ancient instrument which looks like a lute.

*Allah or God**
A wise-looking religious dignitary (sheikh) about sixty years old, his head and beard are silvery white, his complexion slightly pale and his clothes made of white cloth are worn wide and long. He is seated on a majestic throne, and remains motionless most of the time. In front of him there is something like a fine curtain, a thin screen of smoke so that he cannot be seen clearly. His voice so low, his words pronounced with a slow dignity.

Ordinary people, men, women and children

Soldiers

Beautiful maidens

*Isis**

Poor people, peasants, agricultural workers, factory workers, soldiers, students, prostitutes, village barbers, doctors, bankers, traders, pawnbrokers, ministers, heads of state

King Farouk, Anwar El Sadat, the Sphinx, Ronald Reagan, George Bush, Cleopatra, Antony, Nefertiti, Ekhnatoun, Umm Kulthum, Rabia al-Adaweya, Karl Marx, Sigmund Freud*

One-Eyed Man, Benjamin Netanyahu,* Bill Clinton**

Young girls, boy

Child, Other child**

Schoolboy

Clerk

Court attendant

Angels, media representatives

Maat, Isis

*Chief of Police**

* Indicates sepaking parts

The stage is dark. Moses, peace be with him, is advancing through the desert at night. As the light grows he emerges. He looks increasingly exhausted and anxious. His body is bent slightly as though under a load. He stops and looks around like someone who has lost his way. He sits on a sand rock to rest, opens a cloth bag and takes out what looks like a Bible, a flat loaf of dry bread, and a piece of cheese. He chews slowly, muttering to himself with the book held in his hands.

Prophet Moses   It is a long time since I saw him on the mountain. I and my people have followed his orders to the letter. His words in the Bible have been raised higher than all things. He said to us, cut off the foreskin of the male and we did. He said to us, kill the inhabitants of Canaan and Palestine and take their land. We have killed them and have taken their land. He said to us, stone the woman who commits adultery and indeed that's what we have done.

He said to us, I am the Almighty God of the Heavens and the earth and you should not worship anyone else, not even your sacred calf, and we said we have heard thy words and obeyed them and have destroyed the calf. He said to us, of all the people on earth, you alone are my chosen people, and we said of all the gods, thou art our only chosen God.

Moses munches the dry piece of bread with a crackling noise, swallows a little water from a goatskin, and continues his soliloquy.

O God, long, long years have passed since I met you on Mount Sinai, on the sacred mountain which is part of our Promised Land. Is that not true, O God? Did you not tell us in the Old Testament that our Promised Land stretches from the Nile River to the Euphrates?

We have been faithful to our Covenant with you, have cut off the foreskin of all males, and have had them circumcised by law. Not one of them escaped no matter how rigorous the medical campaigns against this harmful operation. Its harm has been proven medically, but we receive our orders from you and not from human beings even if they are doctors. You are the only one we worship and forever. We have kept our pledge to you so why have you not kept your pledge to us? Where is the land you promised us from the Nile to the Euphrates? We have even lost Mount Sinai and now are left only with Palestine. Not the whole of Palestine, only parts of it. The Palestinians have kept parts to this day under the excuse of a United Nations decision. Can a United Nations decision overrule a decision from you, O God? Why do we no longer hear your voice? I long to meet you again the way I did before. I am in great need of your help. My people have sent me to you. I fear their declaring a rebellion against you and going back to the Golden Calf. They love gold, my Lord, and say to me "with gold we can get anything we want, but with you and your God we only get talk!" But do not take them too much to task, O Lord. Forgive them.

Prophet Moses resumes his munching on the dry bread, gazes at the sky with his ailing eyes, to the top of a high mountain, plunged in darkness surrounded in black smoke behind which seems to move a huge phantom, the features of which remain obscure. The sky growls with thunder and flashes with lightning, and a slight rain begins to fall. Moses takes refuge in a cave, stretches out, staring up at the sky, and resumes what he was saying.

I know, O God, that you are angry with your people, with the children of Israel. They have fallen into the clutches of Satan, he whispers peace into their ears, says to them "give away land in exchange for peace." How can he say such things? You know him well, O God, he does not believe in your word. He tells people that it is you who have ordered the massacres of human beings for the Promised Land. People have started listening to his whisperings. They are tired of the successive wars that have taken place since the establishment of Israel and are prepared to evacuate some of the smaller towns on the West Bank in return for peace. But amongst my people there are still men loyal to you, faithful to your Covenant. Among them is your loyal son, Benjamin. His father, Netanyahu, gave him the name of the Prophet Benjamin so that he would remain faithful to his people, imbued with the faith of the prophets who are prepared to kill all men in order to ensure that God's word is fulfilled, for thy words are above all other things and we obey you, O Lord, follow your orders, not those of the United Nations or of any human being, even be it the President of the United States—Bill Clinton.

The heavens quiet down a little. At the other end of the stage, in the distance emerges Jesus Christ, peace be with him. He moves with the gait of a slender youth, eager for an encounter with his Father the Almighty God, after a long absence. He looks up to the high mountain sill plunged in darkness in clouds of black smoke and thick fog. He looks up, stops for a moment, lifts his left hand to the Heavens to his Father on the Mountains with the Bible held up to him in it.

Jesus Christ   Oh, my father, does not your heart soften towards your obedient Son who shed his blood on the cross in order to fulfill your will? Why dost thou deprive me of a chance to meet with you? Does not a loyal son have the right to see his father? At least once in his life before he dies? I have traveled this long and arduous journey to ask for your help. My people have gone astray. The churches are no longer frequented except by women, children, and old people. Men who are still strong or youths are busy making money. Younger women have joined women's "lib", called the feminist movement. This is a disaster, my Father. These women write dangerous books which have spread among women. Almost nobody needs your book, the Bible. Publishing houses are no longer eager to reprint it except for the smaller ones sponsored by some universities mainly for teaching purposes in the departments of religion and history. Can you imagine, O God, that your book has become no more than a relic of past history in which no one is interested except researchers or critics, the majority of whom are women? They have riddled your book with all sorts of criticisms and you have remained silent. These are the women whom you ordered to remain silent, whose voices we never used to hear. If you order me to go back to them I will do so at once. I have come seeking your help. Why dost thou not answer me? O my Father! My Father! I call upon you. Your suffering son is calling upon you, will you not listen to him?

The heavens remain plunged in silence. No thunder, no lightning, not a single movement of a tree leaf. The air is still, the sky is as blue as the sea, and the sea is motionless with not a single wave. It is a single, solid, silent mass of blue. The land is the color of sand like an endless desert stretched out under the sky. The universe is without movement in it as though all things have perished.

Jesus Christ drops to his knees, his head buried in his hands and starts to sob silently, muttering between sniffs.

Jesus Christ   Oh my Father, this torment is greater than any torment I suffered on the cross. I called upon you, my Father, when I hung from the cross, but thou didst not answer me, and now you still keep a silence I cannot understand. O Father, how I yearn for you, for my mother's arms. I want to weep on her chest, ask for her forgiveness. How cruel I was to her. I kept ignoring her for your sake. Yet it is she who gave birth to me, fed me with her milk, and protected me from my enemies. She it was who remained by my side until the last moment when everyone around me had fled, had abandoned me including even You, my Father. Why did you leave me like that when I hung from the cross, bleeding to the last drop of my blood? O Mother!! O Mother, forgive the sins of your son. But I did not feel that you existed. I never heard your voice. My Father ordered you to be silent and spoke in your place. I was small and listened to my Father and my Father used to tell me not to listen to what women say. Yes, Father that is what you said and you did not stop at that. I have your book as a witness, and here it is.

Jesus Christ holds up the Bible between his two hands shaking with emotion, turning over the pages with his long, thin fingers, which keep trembling all the time.

The heavens begin to growl, thunder can be heard coming from high up on the mountain, and rain pours down. Jesus Christ takes refuge in the cave and there he comes upon the Prophet Moses crouching with his arms folded around his knees, busy reading the Bible; they embrace like long lost brothers.

Prophet Moses   Brother Jesus, I heard you asking God Almighty to let you into his presence. Calm down. Here, drink some water (*handing him a goatskin*). I know all about the disaster you are going through, but God will make you triumph over your women enemies and over the men also. You have been patient for centuries; so why not be patient for another day or two? I have asked for a meeting with Almighty God. I sent a fax to Lord Radwan. Peace be with him.

Jesus Christ (*with astonishment*) Fax?! Do you think they have a fax in the Heavenly Kingdom?

Prophet Moses Of course, brother. God possesses the tree of all knowledge. Do you think that he doesn't know about the fax and about all the other human discoveries? You, my son have to send a request by fax, otherwise Lord Radwan will not examine your case.

Jesus Christ Do you have the fax number?

Prophet Moses Yes, here it is.

From between the pages of the Bible, he extracts a slip of paper with a very long number written in it. Jesus starts copying the number into a small notebook he carries with him.

This number is extremely confidential. Don't give it to anyone. God sent it to me with one of his holy angels as I lay in this cave. The angel said to me, "God has given you and the people of Israel exclusive access to this number because you are the chosen people."

Jesus Christ Please, Brother Moses, there is no need to talk about this matter of a chosen people. God is my Father. I am his son and my people are his chosen people.

Prophet Moses pulls the slip of paper angrily out of Jesus' hands before he has time to copy the number written on it.

Prophet Moses Brother, then let your father give you his number! You and your people are always like that. You strike the hand that is held out to help you.

Jesus Christ (*with pride*) What help? We are the ones who give you loans and aid. Your state in its entirety would not have been established had we not carried it on our shoulders. Did we not supply you with the arms you needed to kill the people of Palestine and the Arabs? Even the nuclear weapons which we withhold from everybody else have been made an exception for you. You were wanderers scattered all over the world and we made of you a state like other states even though your state has come to be only shedding blood and continuing to do so despite our objections. What more do you want than what you now have, Brother Moses? The Promised Land from the River Nile to the Euphrates?! That is greed and avarice that exceeds the limits.

Prophet Moses You are an arrogant and conceited young man, my son, who imagines he is the center of the universe. Our state of Israel was established by the will of God, not that of man. If you help us it is to serve your interests in the Middle East. Were it not for our presence in the area you would not have had a place in it, brother. Those differences between us will only benefit our Muslim enemies. Here, swallow a morsel of this. You must be hungry after your long journey.

They crunch pieces of dry bread in unison. Jesus Christ whispers a prayer.

Jesus Christ We thank you, O Lord, for this our daily bread. Forgive us our sins as we forgive the sins of others against us ... Thine is the Kingdom of Heaven, the power and the glory forever and ever ... Amen.

At the other end of the stage, at a distance, the Prophet Muhammad comes into sight, advancing with a slow step, his eyes fixed ahead, the Book of God, the Qur'an carried in one hand, a rosary in the other, circling slowly between his fingers. He moves forward a few more steps before coming to a stop.

Prophet Muhammad Things seem to have changed on this path since the last time I came here. Everything changes. Nothing is eternal, except Allah the Almighty, the above all. It used to lead to al-Medina al-Menawara, and there was a cave to which God led me. The moment I entered it, he told the spider to run to its door and spin threads over it. The infidels walked up and when they saw the cobweb on the door they went their way thinking that no one could be inside. I left the cave. That way God saved me from death with the help of a small spider. Were it not for it I would never have reached al-Medina al-Menawara, and the state of Islam would never have been. Almighty God, ruler of the heavens and the earth, the one and only, thou knowest what lies in our hearts, thou knowest why I have come to you this day asking for your help. The state of Islam and of the Arabs at one time reached from the land of the Parsees to the land between the two rivers, to Syria, Egypt to the countries of the East and the West, to Andalusia in Spain. But the affairs of the Muslims have declined rapidly, their governments are corrupt, the state of Islam has shrunk and continues to shrink so that I fear a day when it will disappear completely from the face of the earth. The countries of Islam and of the Arabs have dropped behind and are most called backward countries. Yet, Western civilization was built on the achievements of Arab civilization. Thou hast endowed us with many riches, for our nation, as you mentioned in your holy book, is the greatest nation on earth. The most important of these riches is oil, of course, but oil has changed from a weapon in our hands to a weapon in the hands of our enemies. Satan whispers in the ears of people saying: "Where is your Almighty Allah, you people of Islam? Why do the Jews and the Christians gain victory over you in every battle? Battle after battle you are defeated; in battle after battle you lost your land, your riches, and your sons. This despite the fact that you are holding on to your religion, on to your morals, and your virtue more than any other people. Your women are veiled and virtuous, whereas the women of the Christians and Jews are not veiled and go around naked." God help us, corruption has not gone that far in our lands. Today I have come to you, O God, to seek your advice in a matter of great urgency that brooks no delay. This family that rules over the land of the Hejaz, the sons of Saud have sown corruption in their land. Their king calls himself the servant of the two sacred cities Mecca and Medina whereas he serves no one but himself. Even the tomb where I was buried is neglected. There is a wall around it which is ready to collapse, but he never stops building palaces for his women and his children. He collects vast sums of money from the pilgrims who visit Allah's sacred dwelling and from the revenues of oil and deposits them in his name in the banks which belong to the Christians and the Jews. He negotiates in secret with the Jews and the Christians against the Muslims and then goes to pray in the mosque without doing his ablutions. O God, he distorts the image of Islam all over the world then says that thou hast forbidden women to drive cars, that it was I who said in one of my sayings despite the fact that I never said anything of the kind. Cars had not been invented in my days and women rode camels. Besides, what difference does it make if it's a car or a camel? At least a car has a roof which protects a woman from sand storms, and brigands, whereas a camel has no roof. Satan has taken advantage of this talk and is busy whispering into the ears of women. But women in our lands do not listen to his whisperings. They are virtuous and chaste, not like the women of the Jews and Christians.

The problem in our countries, O God, is the kings. Kings, once they rule over a village, corrupt it. I visited the King of Saudi Arabia in his sleep and said to him, "Now listen to me, Fahd, Allah has told you to shun corruption. You hoard up silver and gold which belongs to Muslims and yet neglect their needs." But when he woke up in the morning he changed the dream and said that I had visited him in his sleep to tell him that we were pleased with him and with his doings and that agreement with the children of Israel was a good thing since they were people of the Book, and since God had sent down the Torah and the New Testament as a guide for all people. So I have come to you, O God, seeking your help against the tyranny of this Saudi king who has transformed his country into a military base to be utilized by the armies of the enemies of Muslims against them, and I fear that my nation will be no more.

Prophet Muhammad sits down on a small sand rock looking exhausted from his long and difficult journey. Then he stands up before Allah to do his prayers to him, kneels, and prostrates himself four times, before he sits on the rock again, moving his rosary through his fingers in silence, all the time looking up at the heavens as though waiting for some response.

In the cave sit Prophet Moses and Jesus Christ as though watching Prophet Muhammad to see what he will do after they have heard everything he has said to God.

Prophet Moses   Do you believe that God really said to them that they are the best people? This is a lie and purports to God something he never said. And look at what he said about the Jews and the Christians. This man is a dangerous enemy. We must destroy him before he has a chance to finish us off.

Jesus Christ   Brother Moses, calm down and don't let anger take a hold on you. Muhammad has recognized us as people of the Book. He believes that the Torah and the New Testament are God's words, so we can negotiate with him. He is better than other people, who refuse to consider the Torah and the New Testament as coming from God.

Prophet Moses   Negotiate with him? Over what, Brother Jesus? We have no need of him or of his Muslim people. They no longer have any power, any ability to do anything. They have neither money, nor arms, nor knowledge, nor technology.

Jesus Christ   No, we are in need of him, Brother Moses.

Prophet Moses   Of what use to us can he be?

Jesus Christ   Without a doubt he is on our side against Satan, and I am certain that Satan has knowledge of our meeting here. Nothing escapes him. He might even be able to have a meeting with my Father. I know that my Father is careful to ensure that he continues to exist for he cannot conceive of a world without Satan in it.

Prophet Moses   Why, my brother? Why not?

Jesus Christ   You must ask him that question yourself. As for that Devil Satan, I wish he would die at once, but he continues to be lively as ever. We are the ones who have died a thousand deaths.

The heavens start growling. At a distance Satan appears advancing with an energetic youthful stride. Muhammad ceases his prayers as the rain starts to fall, gathers his robe around him quickly, and rushes off looking for shelter. In the cave Jesus Christ welcomes him while Prophet Moses maintains a silence.

Jesus Christ   Brother Muhammad. You will be safe here with your Brother Jesus and Moses.

Prophet Muhammad   We are one family, Brother Jesus, son of the chaste Mother Mary. You are very dear to us, and you too, Brother Moses. Allah mentioned you in the Qur'an a hundred and twenty times.

Prophet Moses   A hundred of them with curses of course.

Jesus Christ   Look who's coming. It's Satan.

Prophet Muhammad   There are two women arriving from the opposite direction. Who are they?

Prophet Moses   One of them looks like Eve, but I do not recognize the other one.

At the far end of the stage emerge Bint Allah (daughter of Allah) and Eve walking side by side, both of them tall, slender, of almost equal height. However, Bint Allah has the features of a young girl of about eighteen, whereas Eve is a young but mature woman of around forty.

They hide behind a cactus fig tree when they spot Satan from a distance as he gazes up to the top of the mountain to the Almighty God hidden by clouds and dark smoke.

Satan   It's finished with me. O God, I am tired of whispering in people's ears. I have decided to tender my resignation to you. I found other work which will bring in lots of money. The job you gave me, God, has tired me out and all I get out of it are curses, so I have written a resignation. I could have sent it to you by fax, but I preferred to come with it myself so that we can make it up between us and forget the hateful past which made me your enemy.

Satan brings out a folded sheet of paper from his pocket and starts reading.

I, the undersigned named Satan the Devil, known as Lucifer, carrier of Light, which is the name bestowed on me by my mother, hereby declare that I am resigning from the post assigned to me by God the Almighty and Most High. I have clarified the reasons for this decision in my resignation, should God desire to examine them, and all I ask of Him is that He look for another Satan to replace me.

Signed, Lucifer

Satan is heard calling out.

Brother Radwan, gate-keeper of Paradise, inform your boss that I deserve to meet him for a few minutes. I know he is busy, but tell him that Satan the Devil wishes to see him this last time and that after that none of you will ever see my face again. Here is my resignation.

Eve and Bint Allah come to a stop. Satan stops them and moves towards them, smiling.

Satan   Welcome Eve. And you, young woman, who are you?

Bint Allah   I am Bint Allah (daughter of Allah).

Satan, at the sound of her name, shows great astonishment, laughs heartily, and strikes the palm of his hand against his forehead. Still laughing he exclaims.

Satan   That is the most beautiful name I have ever heard. Who gave it to you, my girl?

Bint Allah   The authoress.

Satan   What a woman. Even I, Satan, never imagined that Allah could give birth to a girl. He declared in his Book the Torah that his only children are sons and that his sons marry the daughters of people whom they find beautiful. Have you read that verse in the Torah, my girl?

Eve   The version of history we find in the Torah is all wrong. I am Eve. I am here, in my flesh and blood. My mother gave birth to me in the fields. Her labor pains seized upon her while she worked the land so what's this story about my husband giving birth to me from one of his ribs? My mother planted an apple tree in the middle of a field and your Most High God wanted to take all its fruits for himself. He conspired with my husband to chase me away, incited him to be unfaithful to me in exchange for money. He spread rumors describing the tree as sacred rumors, saying that whosoever partook of its fruits would die. I have eaten of it many times without anything ever happening to me. Can a person die from eating an apple, Satan?

Satan   Apples, my lady, are the most delicious of fruits. They bring happiness to the heart and cure the sick. Many a time have I crept through the night to steal the fruit of apple trees, but God on high never caught me.

At this point the heavens begin to growl again. There are peals of thunder, flashes of lightning and rain. Master Radwan appears gradually from behind clouds and layers of smoke.

Master Radwan God in his majesty has had pity on you people of the earth and will accord you an audience. He has no time to meet you one by one; all of you come up at the same time. I received your names by fax and my Lord Master was in a good mood at the time. He was drinking tea with mint after a rich meal of grilled lamb. By the way, did you remember to bring slaughterings with you? My Master accepts only lamb, or veal, or young cow's meat. He refuses anything else. Those of you who have come empty-handed had better go back to where you came from. We have no time to waste with them.

Prophet Moses *(steps forward)* Yes, Master Radwan, I have brought a lamb of the kind which your Most High Master likes best of all.

Jesus Christ *(steps up behind him)* He is my father, Brother Radwan, and a father does not ask his son for slaughtered offerings.

Prophet Muhammad In his Book, the Holy Qur'an, Allah did not ask us to offer him slaughterings. Here, take a look. I have brought the Qur'an with me.

Eve I am a poor woman and your Most High Lord says he sides with poor people.

Bint Allah He is my father, the Imam who married my mother.

Satan Radwan, I am Satan and you cannot prevent me from entering. All I want is to give my resignation.

Prophet Abraham rushes up at this moment to join the small group that stands in line ready for the meeting with the Most High of all gods.

Prophet Abraham Radwan, I am the father of all prophets and I have come on an urgent matter which must be settled before I die.

Behind Prophet Abraham follows a throng of ordinary people, men, women and children, who crowd in behind him, so that Radwan has no chance to shut the door before they get in.

SCENE TWO

The Most High of all gods is seated on a high throne that resembles the throne of an emperor. It is a golden gilt chair adorned with ornate trappings and surrounded by comfortable sofas covered in richly colored materials. Over them hang clusters of red grapes. The majestic figure on the throne wears the garments of an emperor and around him are gathered soldiers standing in rows. One of the soldiers waves a fan made of ostrich feathers back and forth over the head of the emperor-like figure. At a distance can be seen a lake, rivulets of wine and beautiful maidens partly obscured by fine curtains of cloud and smoke. There is also a huge tree from which hang crimson-colored fruits.

The ground is covered in thick carpeting on which are seated the people who thronged in to meet the Most High of all rulers. On his right side stands Master Radwan who undertakes the task of responding to the questions on behalf of his master seated on the throne, except when he receives a sign from him. Then he lapses into a complete silence and the Most High of all gods undertakes to answer in person.

Silence descends on everybody and there reigns an atmosphere of great awe. Prophet Moses sits cross-legged. Next to him in line sits Jesus Christ, Prophet Muhammad, then Abraham. Bint Allah and Eve sit on the other side together with Satan, the goddess Isis and the Virgin Mary. Nothing can be heard except the whisper of the ostrich feather fan as it waves backwards and forwards, cooling the air over the head of the Most High seated on the throne. Three knocks with a hammer are heard signaling the beginning of the session like in court.

Master Radwan   Who of you wishes to begin? Please be brief and to the point. Our Most High has not much time.

Prophet Moses, Jesus, Muhammad and Abraham whisper to one another.

Prophet Muhammad   You begin, Master Abraham. You are the father of all prophets and no one should speak before you.

Prophet Abraham stands up, steps forward, his head bent in respect.

Prophet Abraham   My conscience is stricken and I fear to die before having let out what torments me. During my life I have done many wrongs, all of them in compliance with your orders. I have killed people, and stolen their lands unjustly. Yet, at the same time my faith in you has never been shaken. I wrecked your dwelling and built your altar. I made Sarah slaughter a calf every time you came to our house, made her put bread and ghee on the table, fat on the fire so that you could breathe in the smell of grilling, lay down a finely spun carpet from Abrasheen for you to sit on and bowls made of chamchad wood for you to eat from. When you sat eating under the tree I used to remain standing in front of you. I made sure to find beautiful maidens to please your eyes and to avoid hearing you say angrily: "Why do you always find old crones with one leg or one eye to inflict upon me?" I executed your orders to the letter, at times I questioned your decisions to kill, asked you why we should massacre thousands of people just because one of them refused to obey you? But you never listened to me. You listened only to yourself, worshipped yourself and made us your slaves, forced upon us blind obedience, gave yourself the right to do anything, whereas you should have followed the path of justice and obliged me, since I am your prophet, to follow on it behind you. But you made out of me a killer without a conscience, a traitor with no morals.

You ordered me to abandon my beloved wife and her son, Ishmael, in the desert to die of thirst and hunger and be devoured by hyenas. You had no pity on a poor woman and her small infant, just in order to favor my first wife Sarah. Yet it was Sarah who advised me to marry her slave Hagir. She said to me "I am an old woman and cannot give birth to a child. You need progeny to inherit after you," but after I married Hagir and gave birth to Ishmael she was consumed with jealousy. Then you ordered me to satisfy Sarah's desires, to throw out Hagir and Ishmael into the wilderness. I knew you were being unjust, that You stood up for Sarah because she was rich and possessed many heads of sheep, slaughtered a lamb for you every time you visited us, baked loaves of bread with ghee for you, laid down a carpet from Abrasheem for you and brought you bowls of chamchad wood. Hagir, the slave, owned nothing, so you treated her in the same way as you treated Cain, Adam's son.

You turned your face away from him when he gave you offerings of fruit and vegetables, and welcomed Abel's offerings of young, well-fed sheep. Cain was humiliated and angry, and thus, Master, you sowed hatred between the brothers just because one of them owned herds of sheep whereas the other had nothing. Both of them came forward with offerings, but you accepted the offerings of one and refused those of the other. As a result one brother killed the other. You were responsible for what happened, but you made Cain the 'poor miserable youth' bear the guilt. It looks as though this earth of ours, O Lord, is accursed with the innocent blood you flow over it and which continues to flow. Do you not witness what is happening in our world? Are you not troubled by all the blood being shed in your name, in the name of your Promised Land, in the name of Abraham and his progeny, the sons of Israel? What is it that you will give me in exchange for all this, my Lord? Before I die, can you give me an answer to my question, be it only one word? Please say something. The whole world is attacking me and I do not know where to turn my face. My conscience is a needle thrusting deep into my chest. I do not understand the reasoning which lay behind your promise of land, behind the Covenant you made with us, O Lord. Was it a secret Covenant? Why do you not say anything? This is a public trial witnessed by people and I want them to judge in all justice between us, to declare who is responsible for shedding all this blood, you or I? Why did you promise this land to me, was it in exchange for the heads of sheep and the offerings of roast lamb I proffered to you?

At this point the Most High of all gods raises his hand in opposition to what Abraham said. The look on his face shows anger. But it is a contained anger suitable to his all-powerful sovereignty.

The Most High God   (*in cold anger*) That is enough! Silence him!

Prophet Abraham stops short, prostrates himself on the ground. There is a total silence broken only by the wisp of the ostrich feather fan. One of the soldiers wipes the sweat off the brow of the Most High of all gods with a sterilized piece of gauze wetted in drops of fragrant water poured from a silver container.

One of the attendants in the court rushes up to Master Radwan carrying the three holy Books in his hands. Radwan opens the first Book, takes a sip of water from a crystal vessel, clears his throat and speaks in clear full tones like a judge in court. He strikes the silver table with a hammer provided with a golden end shaped like the head of a cobra to silence the mutterings and whisperings of people who were following the procedures, for at that particular moment some people who happen to be passing by erupt on the scene. They are a motley crowd composed of poor people on their way to work, men and women, peasants and agricultural laborers, men and women workers in the factories, soldiers, students, prostitutes, village barbers who do circumcision, doctors who do abortion, together with a sprinkling of bankers, traders, pawnbrokers, ministers and even heads of state, as well as people from other professions. All of them sit down on the carpeting laid over the ground. Amongst them can be seen the faces of people well known in history, famous men and women, artists who have died or are still living, as well as kings, and emperors from past ages, or even contemporary times. Recognizable are King Farouk, one-time King of Egypt, but now dead. Anwar El Sadat, one time President of Egypt, now also dead, the Sphinx, Ronald Reagan, George Bush, Cleopatra and Antony, Nefertiti and Ekhnatoun, Umm Kulthum the famous singer of the East, Rabia al-Adaweya, a woman founder of the Islamic Sufi sect, Karl Marx, Sigmund Freud and others from the East and the West. Eve and Bint Allah sit in the front row. As the mutterings and whisperings continue, Eve leans towards Bint Allah.

Eve   Do you know why he gave him this promise of land? In exchange for what?

Bint Allah   In exchange for what?!

Master Radwan bangs on the table with his hammer to stop the muttering going on. There is silence.

Master Radwan   My Most High Lord has delegated me to respond to Prophet Abraham's question. In accordance with the instructions of our Lord President I shall read the passages in the Holy Torah, which deals with the promise of land made to Prophet Abraham. This court is the highest instance of justice. Above it there exists no higher instance. We cannot decide anything without recourse to the sacred texts in the heavenly Books.

Master Radwan puts on his spectacles. From them there hangs a golden chain which reaches down his chest.

He flips over the pages in the Torah.

Master Radwan   Yes gentlemen, I am looking for the verse dealing with this matter of the Promised Land. Ah, here it is. And God said to Abraham, "I, Jehovah the Almighty, do bestow upon you this land to hand down in inheritance. It reaches from the river of Egypt to the River Euphrates."

Master Radwan stretches his hand out to a glass on the table and takes a sip of water. One of the men sitting in the audience is dressed in a military uniform and wears a black patch over one of his eyes. He rubs his hands together with satisfaction whispers in the ear of his neighbor, a man who bears a very close resemblance to Benjamin Netanyahu, Prime Minister of Israel.

The One-Eyed Man   (*looking delighted*) Do you see, Benjamin? We must fight a war of extermination against Egypt and Iraq. The word of the Most High God is in the sacred Torah. We have not given him his due. We have not reached even as far as the River Jordan, although he gave us the land from the Nile to the Euphrates!

Benjamin (Netanyahu)   (*nods his head with approval*) Yes, yes, you are right, Moshe.

In the row just in front of Benjamin Netanyahu sits an American. He has the face of Bill Clinton, President of the United States; he turns half backwards to address Netanyahu in a whisper.

Bill Clinton   I beg of you, Benjamin. Postpone everything just for another two weeks until the elections are over. We have to win against Bob Dole and if you help me to do that, I will give you a helping hand in the future. Don't forget that we are partners.

Master Radwan bangs with his hammer and silence reigns. The voice of a small girl rings out from between the rows.

Master Radwan All that land from the Nile to the Euphrates God gave to the children of Israel!! Why?

Voices of many young girls, boys, women, and men clamor, "Why?" in unison.

Why? Why? For what reason?

Master Radwan bangs loudly with his hammer.

Master Radwan Because they are his chosen people and God the Most High has said so in the Torah.

Prophet Muhammad (*Raises his hand from where he sits in the front row among the other prophets and important personalities. He stands up to speak without prior permission from Master Radwan.*) Master Radwan, the Jews are not the chosen people of Allah. We, the Arabs, are the best of nations born amongst the people of the earth. That is what the text says in the Holy Qur'an.

Master Radwan lays the Torah aside, picks up the Qur'an, flips through and stops at a page.

Master Radwan No, Prophet Muhammad. Look into the Qur'an and you will find that Allah said to the children of Israel, "I have preferred you to all people." He said that not only once, but several times. Go through the Qur'an carefully, Prophet Muhammad.

Prophet Muhammad I agree, Brother Radwan. I know that Allah said that in the Qur'an. The children of Israel, like the Christians, are people of the Book who believe in Allah and are not like the unbelievers and worshippers of idols. Allah asked us to believe in the three Books which he sent down as a guide and a light for all people. But I am the last of all prophets and the Qur'an is the final word of Allah. In it he said to us, you are the finest of all nations created in the world. The Jews rebelled against the Almighty and Most High God many times and worshipped other gods, including the calf.

Muffled laughter is heard amidst the audience, especially coming from the children and the schoolboys and schoolgirls, who occupy a more distant corner of the court area. One of the children laughs out loud exclaiming, "A calf? Is that possible?"

Master Radwan bangs down with his hammer.

Master Radwan Prophet Muhammad, I did not give you permission to speak. Please wait for your turn. The word is now with Prophet Moses. Please go ahead, Master Moses.

But before Prophet Moses starts to speak Bint Allah stands up, raising her hand.

Bint Allah We have not heard an explanation, Master Radwan, to what happened to Hagir and her child Ishmael, or to the question of the Promised Land reaching from the River Nile to the Euphrates, or to why God ordered the children of Israel to kill all the women prisoners among the people of Canaan and Palestine who were not virgins, and at the same time hand over all the virgins to the soldiers so that they could rape them.

A deep silence falls over the people gathered in the court. They bend their heads in shame. Mutterings and whisperings travel through the rows of men and women. Eve stands up and starts to speak.

Eve Master Radwan, the child Ishmael and his mother Hagir faced great tribulation in the desert until they reached a place where people dwelt. There Hagir worked hard in the fields to keep her son. Yet, when the son grew up, Abraham went looking for him, found him, and tried to take him away from his mother by force. Both the mother and the son refused to be separated and what happened? The Most High of gods ordered Abraham to kill his son Ishmael. Was there no other way of pleasing your God except to slaughter your son?

Abraham raises his head bent low between his knees and looks up. He looks old, exhausted.

Prophet Abraham   God used to ask us to slaughter offerings. Every time we asked for his help we had to sacrifice a slaughtered animal. He loved the smell of slaughtered meat. Poor people who had neither cattle nor sheep often slaughtered their sons and daughters to avoid his anger. The slaughtering of a sheep or an ewe replaced the sacrifice of a son or daughter. When God asked me to slaughter my son Ishmael I asked him, why, O God? Here is a sheep I offer to you instead of my son, but he was very angry and said to me I am the Highest of all Gods and I gave you the land and you do not want to give me what I ask of you in return?! I feared that he would take away the land and kill my son himself if I refused to do it.

Abraham holds his head between the hands and weeps in a choked voice.

Prophet Abraham   O my God, thou art cruel, with a heart of stone. You had no pity on me, despite my tears. I beg of you, Master Radwan. Why did he never calm down except when he saw blood being shed? The spouse of Prophet Moses witnessed God's anger and how he wanted to kill her husband, although Moses was even more obedient to him than I was and never once questioned him as I sometimes used to do. Seeing God so angry she wanted to save her husband. Her husband said to her, "God is in a bad mood and must be shown blood to calm down." She had neither a calf, nor a lamb, nor even a small chick. So she took hold of her son and cut off his foreskin. Blood ran from him and thus God calmed down and drew back the idea of killing Moses.

Bint Allah   Cutting off the foreskin is a crime against human beings. Master Radwan, please ask your Most High of all gods why he imposed circumcision on his chosen people in exchange for the Promised Land, promised them land if they promised to circumcise their sons. What is the relation between land and cutting the part of the human body?

Master Radwan responds in an irritable tone of voice.

Master Radwan   I did not give you permission to talk. Please wait your turn.

At this juncture the Most High of all gods lifts his hand in a slow movement, indicating to Master Radwan that he should be silent. Then, speaking in a voice which resembles the rumbling of thunder:

The Most High God   Cutting off the foreskin is a symbol of obedience and submission to me, a duty to be fulfilled by all my slaves.

Silence prevails for a moment, followed by mutterings. Most of those present seem unconvinced by this answer. There are voices of protest raised, especially among the male children. One of them weeps chokingly, hiding his face in his hands, and turns away from the other children. A child sitting next to him whispers in the ear of his neighbor.

Child   The village barber circumcised him and instead of just cutting off the foreskin, cut off the whole head.

Other Child   My wound continued to bleed for days and I almost died. I spent two weeks in bed unable to walk.

Master Radwan bangs down with his hammer and once more there is silence.

Bint Allah   How can you cut off part of a child's body just as a sign that obedience and submission to you has been ensured!? How can your ego take you to such extreme?!

There are signs of anger among the people gathered in the court. Master Radwan bangs with his hammer. Some of the soldiers move in closer to maintain order and everyone is silent again.

Prophet Abraham   O God, we worship you and pray to you, but you do not worship anyone else except yourself. That is your right and no one is allowed to question it. Nevertheless, once you have accorded yourself this right it requires that you oblige us to be just in whatever we do. Instead, you have ordered us to kill and to be unfaithful to our women. If you intend to burn me in Hell, then do it now. I prefer hellfire to the flames which are consuming my heart and my conscience.

Prophet Abraham collapses and loses consciousness. A number of soldiers gather round him, lift him up and carry him out of the court. There is a commotion which subsides as soon as the bangs of the hammer resound.

Master Radwan   It's your turn to speak, Prophet Moses

Prophet Moses is sitting with bent head looking miserable. He lifts his head with an effort, stands up hesitating as though reluctant to speak. He pronounces his words falteringly, choosing them with caution.

Prophet Moses   Master Radwan. My intention in coming here today was to ask God about his promise to give us the lands extending from the Nile to the Euphrates, to remind him that so far he has given us only Palestine, and not even all of Palestine but only parts of it, that we are still fighting every day to take possession of them. The war goes on without a stop and we have suffered a lot due to it. We would never have triumphed over the Arab and the Muslim armies were it not for the support given to us by our beneficent Lord God, were it not for the military and financial aid accorded to us by friendly states and God-fearing peoples who believe in the Holy Book, in the Old and the New Testaments, both testaments and covenants of our Almighty God. When God promises, he always fulfills his pledge; else there would be no difference between the covenants of God and those of men. What my father Abraham said before me has caused me to think, has opened my eyes to things of which I was ignorant. It has reminded me of the tribulations of tragedies through which I and my wife were made to live. I have always obeyed my God blindly, without question. He ordered me to go back to Egypt to enact my magic in front of Pharaoh. But when I was on my way to him, in the dark of night God tried to kill me, and I was never ever to understand why he tried to do that, when he tried to strike me in the back at a time when I was obeying what he ordered me to do.

The Most High God waves his hand in an angry gesture towards Master Radwan and Prophet Moses drops silent.

The Most High God   You aroused my anger, Moses. You argued with me, tried to escape and to avoid doing what I ordered you to do, whereas I am your Almighty God. I created you, gave you life of my own free will, and I have the right to take it away whenever I so desire.

Master Radwan   That is the right of Allah, our Almighty God, Master Moses.

Prophet Moses   I am attentive to what my master says and obey only him. That was the only time I lived to escape and it was because Pharaoh was preparing to kill me.

The Most High God   And what did I do to Pharaoh because of that Moses? Did I not reap on him the most terrible vengeance, not only on him but on the whole army of Egypt also? Did I not drown Pharaoh and his army in the sea? In fact, I took revenge on all the people of Egypt because of you, Moses, and your people. Radwan, read what I said in my Book to the people who are here as to remind them.

Master Radwan   (*reading from God's Book*) And we saved Moses and all those who were with him, but left the others to drown. Verily these are the true words of Allah.

The Most High God   Radwan, read out to them what I did to the people of Egypt.

Master Radwan   (*reading*) And we made the floods, and the locusts, and the lice, and the frogs, and blood to descend upon them, to teach them a lesson, but they were too proud to learn, and were criminal in their ways.

The Most High God   These are my words in the Qur'an as sent down to the Muslims. In this Book I mentioned your name Moses one hundred and twenty times. How many times did I mention the children of Israel, Radwan? Read out to them, Radwan, so that they be reminded.

Master Radwan   (*reading*) And we sent the book to the children of Israel, sent them prophets and wise words, gave them the good things of the earth and privileged them above all people. Children of Israel, remember the blessings I bestowed upon you that I privileged you above all other peoples. Verily these are the true words of Allah.

The Most High God   How many times, Radwan, have I repeated these words?

Master Radwan   Many a time my Lord. Many times, my Lord, and they are all written down here in the Holy Qur'an.

Prophet Moses   Almighty God, I do not deny.

The Most High God   (*interrupting him*) How can you deny any of this, Moses, when I have never stopped mentioning you and your people even in the book I sent down to the Muslims? I forced the Muslims to believe in you as a Prophet, as an emissary sent by me, to believe in the Torah and the New Testament, just as they believe in the Qur'an.

Prophet Moses   Almighty God, I do not deny.

The Most High God   Be silent, Moses. I do not want to hear your voice. Is that how you let yourself be led, by people who refused to believe in the blessings bestowed upon them, and instead followed behind Satan?

Prophet Moses   Almighty God I ...

The Most High God   Not another word else I shall take back the land which you took from the Palestinian people. Besides, why have you occupied the Golan Heights in Syria? Did my Covenant with you include land in Syria? And why do you covet land on the River Jordan? Did I mention the Jordan River in the Torah, Radwan?

Master Radwan   No, my Lord, there is no mention of the Jordan River or of the Golan Heights, only the River Nile and the Euphrates.

The Most High God   Whose turn is it now? I want to be over quickly with this absurd farce. It is indeed no more than an unacceptable farce that I should be seated here listening to all this nonsense. Is this the result of my belief in democracy, Radwan? It is as though the beings I created out of mud cannot be made to possess a mind, must be ruled over by a dictatorship, by brute force! Thus are human beings. They fear but have no shame.

Master Radwan   Almighty God, those who know the meaning of shame are no more. It's now the turn of our Lord Jesus, son of Mary.

Jesus Christ steps forward with the enthusiasm born of youth, and its warmth, his arms opened wide as though in readiness for an embrace, but the Father

God seated on his throne stares at him coldly. Jesus Christ confines himself to a kiss planted on the cheek of his father whose facial muscles contract in displeasure. He pulls out a silk handkerchief and wipes his cheek as though removing spit. Jesus Christ makes an effort to control himself after his initial enthusiasm.

Jesus Christ   I do not know why you refuse to recognize me as your son, whereas my mother now sits amongst the people out there.

Jesus Christ turns his head towards the people sitting on the ground, searching amongst them for his mother, the Virgin Mary. Her face emerges from the rows. She resembles the painting in the churches which show her carrying her child Jesus. By the side appears a picture of Isis, the ancient Egyptian goddess. In her arms she carries her son, Horus. There is a great resemblance between them and the two infants also look like one another. Isis carries the sun on her head whereas the Virgin Mary carries a divine crown.

Virgin Mary   My son, your father came to me in the dark of night dressed in the clothes of an angel. My father was a man whom everybody respected but my mother could not bear children. She prayed to God to make her give birth to a child, promised to give him up to the service of God in the temple. My mother became pregnant with child and gave birth to me, a girl. Nevertheless, she took me to the temple in the fulfillment of her vow so I would be consecrated to the service of God. One night while I was deep in the worship of God I was visited by an angel who did with me what a husband does with his wife. When he noticed that I was trembling with fear he comforted me, said that he was the spirit of God and had been sent by him to bear his son who later would become a prophet. I was overcome with fright and fled from the temple, and from my village, and I lived in an abandoned house until one day, as I lay under a palm tree, the labor pains descended on me and I gave birth to my child. After that I suffered a lot moving from one village to the other, from one town to the other. People kept humiliating me and my father. They said to me, "Daughter of Haroun, your father was not an evil man, nor was your mother a whore," and there was nothing I could find to answer them. I was silent until one day it was you who spoke, my son.

Jesus Christ   Yes, my mother. I used to address people and used to speak to my father, but I neglected you, never said anything to you. Even when I was on the cross I saw you standing near me weeping, but I ignored your presence and your tears and went on addressing my father, went on calling upon him. Society forced this behavior on me. It is patriarchal and honors only the father. It has no respect for women. I tried to defend them, but I failed. The men would violate a woman's body and call her a whore. They would stone her to death. I said to them, "Let him who is without fault throw stones at her."

Virgin Mary   Yes, my son, you said that and even more, but your father abandoned you on the cross and left you to die. Ah my son, my heart was riven apart over you when you were a youth, and when you were a child, and an infant with no father.

Virgin Mary's voice can be heard sobbing quietly before dropping silent. Eve, who is sitting next to her, caresses her shoulder.

Jesus Christ   Father, I came to you today with a request. I want you to refute the tales and stories mentioned in the New Testament which no one with some reason can believe. Tales like the one about women, about the unrepentant adulteress who rode on Satan and mocked at you until you plunged a sword into her and made her blood flow over the heavens. Who is that woman, Father? Feminists these days do not cease asking questions. They have studied ancient history, the history of Egypt and Babel. You say that Babel is the adulterous woman. How can a city become an adulterous woman? Feminists say that in the city of Babel lived the Mother of all mothers, the ancient female goddess who gave birth to Adam and Eve and to all human beings. That you killed the Mother of all mothers, the ancient goddess, Babel, usurped the throne of the city, and then described her as a fearsome adulteress who rode astride Satan. But what you feared most of all was the tower of Babel. You ordered that it be destroyed, that what the people had erected by their labor be brought to the ground. You spread confusion amongst them, made them unable to understand one another, made them fight one another, upset the whole narrative course of history, made that Adam the man give birth to Eve from his rib and thus denied the existence of an ancestral mother in history. You punished Eve, made her bear the guilt of original sin. You justified war for no reason other than self-worship, used the Jews to exterminate the people of Palestine. The wars named Crusades were carried out in your name; the colonial and neo-colonial wars were and still are being carried on in your name. George Bush carried the Bible in his hands when he declared the Gulf War, whereas it was a war for oil that continues until today. International laws stipulate that all land and the natural resources which lie in it are the property of the nations, of the people who live on it. How can the laws made by humans be more just than the laws created by you, my Father, whereas you are our Almighty God? The laws of God are supposed to be more just than the laws made by human beings. The international law passed by the United Nations Organization stipulates that women are equal to men and should enjoy full human rights, including the right to own their bodies. You made men rule over women, control them, possess their bodies. So where is your justice in all this, Father who made me die on the cross for him?

Jesus Christ kneels, holds his head in his hands, and weeps quietly. There is a complete silence broken only by the wisp of the ostrich feather fan. A soldier wipes the sweat off the brow of the Most High God who pushes him away angrily. The soldier moves back respectfully.

The Most High God   (*speaking in a sad tone*) My son, justice changes from age to age. You cannot compare rules of justice today with what they were twenty centuries ago. What is considered unjust today might have been seen as just in that country or city. Judgments vary with time and place, my son.

There are mutterings among the people gathered in the court and some of them raise their hands to speak. Master Radwan knocks the table with his hammer. Bint Allah raises her hand, but Master Radwan ignores her.

Master Radwan   It is still your turn, Jesus Christ, or have you finished what you wanted to say? Do you want to add something?

Jesus Christ lifts his head, his eyes full of tears.

But Father, you insisted that your judgments are eternal and do not change with time or place.

The Most High God   My son, I have rules that do not change, that remain stable and others which can be changed. My three Books have events and stories that are true and happened in the lives of people, and others which are symbolic. For example, the tower of Babel was a symbol of corruption and that is why I ordered it to be destroyed. However, I did not destroy the Eiffel Tower in Paris, nor the Pyramids in Egypt, nor the skyscrapers in New York, although they are all higher than the tower of Babel.

Jesus Christ   But then, my Father, in your Books how can we tell which stories are true from the others which are symbolic, and how can we differentiate between your eternal, unchangeable judgments and those that can be changed?

The Most High God   It is the task of human interpretation.

Jesus Christ   That means we can only understand your word through human interpretations whereas all of them are either different, or contradictory. If human beings are to interpret the word of God it can only mean that they understand things more clearly than God and that is not possible. Also, if God's words carry more than one meaning it signifies that they cannot be his words. My Father, you throw a heavy load on the shoulders of human beings when you ask them to differentiate between the true and the symbolic, the eternal and the transient. That is why people whose task it is to interpret the texts fight with one another, and shed blood. They insist that what they say is a true expression of your word and emanates from you. That means that your word is not something exact, something we can refer to as true. The mind of human beings is inferior compared to yours and so you must forgive them for any confusion, any inability to understand your words and explain them. The reason of God is greater than any other reason and his word should be clearer than that of all human beings.

Master Radwan gives a few knocks with his hammer.

Master Radwan   Your turn is over, Jesus Christ. You have taken up other people's time.

Jesus Christ   I apologize for that, but I have one last question I want to ask you, Father. Did you create the human being before you created animals or did animals come first? We do not know because your words in the Book are contradictory. And why have you assumed the body of man? Did you Yourself exist before You created the universe, and where were you? In another universe? These days more than one universe has been found to exist, as well as other systems bigger than the solar system, or the moon mentioned in your Book. We are at a loss, my Father.

The Most High God   The reason of the human being is lacking, my son. It is incapable of visualizing my existence away from time and place. I exist outside the limits of place and time, outside the limits of any universe which has been or can be discovered. This way of visualizing is, of course, beyond the human mind, but millions of people all over the world, to this day, believe that I created the world, that I existed before it came to be, so why is that, my son?

Jesus Christ   I have no answer to that, my Father.

Silence prevails in the court. People are deep in thought. Even the fan is motionless in the hand of the soldier. The Most High God looks exalted, triumphant. Bint Allah raises her hand asking to speak.

Master Radwan   It's not your turn.

Bint Allah   Millions of people continue to believe because they are afraid of being punished in this world or in the next, of being burnt in hellfire, of being chased out of their land, or killed because they have disobeyed Allah, or the Imam or God's representatives on earth. Millions of people in Germany believed in Hitler and the Nazis, millions of people in England believed in Thatcher, millions of people in Israel believed in Golda Meir and Benjamin Netanyahu, millions in the United States believe in George Bush, millions of people in Iraq believed in Saddam Hussein, and millions in Egypt believed in Sadat. In all countries of the world millions of people have believed in bloody tyrants in fear of torture or prison, or in fear of being accused of apostasy, of atheism, of communism, of licentiousness, or of feminism. Leaders of the world declare war holding the Torah, or the Bible, or the Qur'an between their hands. They carry your Books, my Lord, and fight wars from Israel to South Africa, from Asia to Latin America. My Lord, you have made wars of plunder sacred and if an atomic war breaks out in the world, it will be in your name.

Master Radwan bangs loudly on the table with his hammer.

Master Radwan   Please be silent or else we will expel you from the court by force!

Eve   Allow her to speak. This is a democratic hearing.

Virgin Mary   Let her speak. She expresses the opinions of the majority here, the silent majority.

Sounds of mutterings go through the gathering. The voices of women, small schoolchildren, youths, and men rise above the mutterings.

A Chorus of Voices   Let her continue, Master Radwan. We join our voice to hers.

Master Radwan   Respected ladies, gentlemen time is short and is almost over. Prophet Muhammad has not yet spoken and this young lady is encroaching on his time. Prophet Muhammad, please begin.

Prophet Muhammad stands up and takes a few dignified steps forward before coming to a stop.

Prophet Muhammad   I would like to start by thanking our benefactor and Lord, creator of the universe, for sitting with us, all this long time despite the many things he has to deal with and for listening to these different opinions with such an openness of mind and without anger. Whereas it is within his power, if he so wishes, to transform this court into hellfire. He is the most compassionate, the most merciful who unfolds us in his mercy and in the kindness of his great heart. I have come here, O Lord, my benefactor to complain to you against King Saud, who has sown widespread corruption in the sacred land of the Hejaz and has allowed foreign soldiers to step over it with their boots and fight against the Muslims. I wish to thank the young girl who preceded me in mentioning this king and other kings and rulers who, in your name most glorious and Almighty God, have caused much blood to be shed, have seized lands and money, whereas you have nothing in common with them or with what they say. They do that in my name too, I who am your prophet and your slave, although I am innocent of what they impute to me. They distort what is said in Your Book the Holy Qur'an and interpret it to their likes. They spread sayings which they impute to me, although they have been branded as they change the place and time of the sayings which I did pronounce. I have a saying in which I say to them, "You know best how to deal with the affairs of your life," but they neglect what I said. They oppress their women in thy name, God Almighty, and in mine also. In my time, that is sixteen centuries ago, I did not impose the veil on women. I ruled that she had the right to choose her husband and to divorce him if she no longer wanted to see his face. But they oppress women and poor people, hoard up gold and silver and the money coming in from oil. They negotiate in secret with the enemies of Islam and have distorted its image to the extent that their Sheikh ibn al-Baz published a book in which he said that the face of a woman is obscene and should be covered with the exception of half of her eyes. He said that it was I who had made this ruling. I have nothing in common with that man. He is supported by the authorities in Saudi Arabia. He made a laughing stock of us amongst the peoples of the world by refusing to recognize the knowledge we get from science, and insisting that the earth is flat and not round. All these things he insists emanate from you, the Almighty, and from me, whereas Islam is built on reason, on science, and knowledge. The first verse you sent down to me, O God, was read in the name of you, Most High of all gods, who taught us with the pen. The Almighty is much greater than they depict him to be. How I wish I could go back to them, my Lord God, confront them with their lies and save my nation, save the Muslims from their evil. They have become corrupt, have sown corruption, and have caused the Muslims to suffer defeat after defeat, so that they are now at the rear of the world when at one time they stood right at the front carrying the torch of civilization and science.

I have come to you this day, My Lord God, with a plea. The world today is in direst need for a prophet to be sent on your behalf to save them from being lost, from those who lead them astray.

The Most High God is silent, plunged in deep thought. He signals to Master Radwan with his hand. They consult in whispers. Master Radwan returns to where he was seated. A murmuring goes round. He bangs with his hammer and silence is restored.

Master Radwan   The Most High God agrees to what Prophet Muhammad has said. All the kings and rulers on earth, in the West and East, in the North and South, are corrupt and the world is in need of a new prophet to be sent by him. However, this matter requires time to decide. Our Almighty God requires some time to choose one from amongst his prophets to be his emissary to the people of the twenty-first century. My Lord Master will be holding a closed meeting with all his Prophets and emissaries, starting with Prophet Abraham right through to Prophet Muhammad. We shall give you, if our Lord Benefactor wills, his name immediately as he has been chosen. And now our meeting is over and I wish you all ...

Bint Allah stands up and interrupts Master Radwan.

Bint Allah   I have not yet been given permission to speak, Master Radwan.

Eve   Why can't we attend this meeting, Master Radwan? Why should all prophets and emissaries be men? Is there not a single woman good enough to be a prophet?

There is a wave of murmuring in the court. A schoolboy stands up. He is carrying an ancient-looking musical instrument. He looks intelligent and rather mischievous.

Schoolboy   And we haven't heard Satan. Is he not the origin of all evil in the world?

The schoolchildren laugh. A group of them stand in unison and cry out: We want to hear Satan! We want to hear Satan! *The schoolboy who asked the question plays on his musical instrument.*

There is disorder in the court and a commotion. The audience bursts into laughter and heads turn round looking for Satan. Master Radwan bangs on his hammer to restore order.

Satan stands holding up the paper on which he has written his resignation. There is silence. Everybody listens.

Satan   This is a meeting that will go down in history, Master Radwan. It is the first time that the Most High God has listened to our voices. He never listened to anyone except himself, never saw anyone except Himself, never worshipped anyone but himself. Worship of oneself requires that one be responsible since responsibility is linked to power and cannot be separated from it. If the Most High God is all powerful, if his power rises above any other power, if his omnipotence is greatest and permits him to do anything then He must be responsible, and his responsibility must also be the greatest. This is justice and it conforms to reason. Justice is a clear and simple logic of things. Since the Highest God is the highest of all in wisdom and the greatest of all minds his logic should be the most just and the easiest to understand. The words of Allah must be more just and easier to understand than those of human beings.

But my Lord God, your words in the three Holy Books were lacking, they needed human beings to explain them to people. They also needed to be translated. Your words in the three Books contradicted each other. You did not make justice and reason the highest virtues. The greatest of virtues for You was to worship no other god. The greatest sin for You was infringement of this rule, of an undivided worship of You, the single God and Almighty. In the Qur'an it is said, "Allah forgives all sins except that of sharing Him." That is how, my Lord, you throw overboard justice and reason. In your eyes, whosoever did not worship you became an apostate, a non-believer whom people had the right to kill. You proclaimed that you know everything that goes on among human beings. But you know nothing about them since you are unable to communicate with them directly, otherwise you would not have sent prophets and emissaries. You tried to hide your incapacity by making things obscure, by using symbols, or miracles, or sorcery to influence people. Pharaoh, my Lord, had more sorcerers than you ever had, and had more snakes than Prophet Moses. You did not trust your Prophet Abraham to obey you so he sacrificed his son. You could have found out what you wanted to know without obliging him to slaughter his innocent boy. You turned him into a bad example for fathers and husbands. Fatherhood and marital fidelity were brought low through fear of you. You could have tested Abraham's loyalty in a manner which would have made him more humane, deepen his sense of fatherhood, strengthened his attachment to his wife and his son. But you put worship and religious ceremonials above humanitarian principles. It is true that sometimes you would talk differently and say people cannot be forced to believe, but on the whole you stood against free thought and knowledge. In your Book the Torah you tried to monopolize the tree of knowledge, although in the Qur'an you made a retreat and did not mention its name at all. You just called it the tree, but you remained opposed to knowledge and reason. There are many differences between the three Books. This has confused people and divided them into religious sects, groups, and movements. They fight one another in your name; carry one of your Books in one hand and a sword or a bomb in the other. But most important of all, in the three Books you have depicted me as the enemy of all people as being responsible for all the evil in the world. How can I be responsible when you are the one who possesses the power, the arms, the knowledge, the media, the heavens and the earth, everything? My Lord, with all your power, your omnipotence, you could have prevented the shedding of all that blood in Palestine, you could have stopped the accumulations of atomic and other weapons in the arsenals of the United States, of Israel, of Russia, England, France, and China. These military governments with their atomic and other weapons are the source of corruption in the world, not poor Satan who does not even carry a sword, has never carried a weapon, any weapon. What fault did I commit? Was it my refusal to bow before Adam? How can I bow to someone who is corrupt? In your Book you admit that Adam was corrupt. Nevertheless, you made him your successor, your plenipotentiary delegated to rule the earth. The angels, all the angels, and not I alone, rebelled. They said, "Do you designate he who will sow corruption on earth, whereas we do not cease to lift our praises to you?" You admitted to that in the Qur'an and if he who is corrupt is made to rule, to be your viceroy, what can we expect to happen? Will not corruption become widespread?

When we ask you why you did that your answer was that is my will, my desire and in that I am free. But freedom, my Lord, means to be responsible and if Almighty God is not responsible for his acts then who is? The people who massacre innocent inhabitants in Palestine or elsewhere are no more than the descendants of corrupt rulers, descendants of Adam and of those who followed after him. You sent Jesus, the son of Mary, her virtuous son but he suffered torture and died on the cross. You admitted that in your Book, the Bible, but denied it in your Book, the Qur'an. Did you feel that the killing of your emissary would raise doubts in people's minds as to your powers? Injustices and corruption breed further injustices and corruption in a never-ending succession. And this is what happened on earth so that all lands have lived in war and were drowned in blood. You made the minority which possesses arms and money rule over the vast majority of people who possess neither arms, nor money. You made men rule over women, legitimized their acts of unfaithfulness and imposed marital fidelity on women alone. You, my Lord, encouraged ignorance and ambiguity, and opposed knowledge. Every step human beings made on the path to more knowledge was forced upon by you, and every war in history was launched in your name. Every man or woman who opposed You was threatened to be burnt by fire or to face death. After all that, my Lord, you expect people to love you. Love and fear cannot dwell together in the heart. I have come this day carrying my resignation with me from the past you forced upon me. I have been the alibi, the excuse which corrupt rulers have used to explain the crimes they commit starting with Adam right down to the Saudi King Fahd or Benjamin Netanyahu in Israel.

Satan approaches the throne of the Most High God, bows respectfully, hands him the resignation, turns round, and walks out of the court. His eyes are brimming with tears. All eyes are fixed on him, filled with awe and astonishment. There is a prolonged silence. The Most High God signals with his hand to Master Radwan. One of the soldiers walks up to him carrying his spectacles on a tray of gold. The Most High God puts on the spectacles which look different from those worn by human beings. He reads Satan's resignation in silence, then throws it on to the tray carried by the soldier who withdraws from the court.

The Most High God signals to Master Radwan. They consult for a moment in whispers then Radwan goes back to his seat.

Master Radwan   The Most High God has instructed us to end the meeting. You are all required to leave, except for the prophets and emissaries whom we wish to remain behind. We will be holding the closed summit meeting after the interval.

SCENE THREE

At the summit meeting presides the Most High God, seated on his throne as before. The prophets and emissaries are seated in a semi-circle. Master Radwan organizes the proceedings, his hand poised on the hammer. At his side is the clerk ready to take notes. The room is luxurious; it looks like the room of a palace. Hanging from the ceiling is a crystal chandelier commonly seen in the palaces of emperors and kings.

The curtain rises and most of the prophets and emissaries mentioned in the three Holy Books are present. Abraham, Moses, Jesus, and Muhammad are seated looking dignified; Abraham in the middle with Moses on his right; Jesus at his left and Muhammad next to him. Muhammad and Jesus converse in quiet tones.

Prophet Muhammad   Our benevolent God was indeed very tolerant and was a great example to us in his respect for different opinions. He it is, who has said belief cannot be forced on people. Let those who wish to be believers believe, and let those who do not want to be believers be free not to believe. People who kill in the name of Islam distort its true image and help our enemies to undermine it. In the West, Islam has become the principal enemy after the collapse of communism.

Jesus Christ   Yes, Brother Muhammad, they need an enemy to wage war and produce weapons. Can you imagine a world without enemies?

A world without Satan? After Satan has resigned what will the world be like, Brother Muhammad?

On the other side Prophet Abraham and Prophet Moses are whispering to one another.

Prophet Abraham   What your people are doing in Israel does not please God. He allotted the land of Palestine to us in accordance with his promise in the Torah, but that was thousands of years ago. So how can they continue to massacre the Palestinians with such savagery? You have aroused everybody against you, even the racist, imperialist government of France. Do you know that Jacques Chirac has become sympathetic to the Arabs and supports an independent state for the Palestinians? Didn't you hear the news on the radio yesterday?

Prophet Moses   This is no more than the struggle between France and America over the Middle East and its oil. Of course I do not agree with that Netanyahu, he exaggerates his supremacy over the Palestinians and encourages the establishment of illegal settlement in the occupied territories, and this blocks progress towards peace which we need even more than the Arabs if Israel is to exist in an atmosphere of security, rather than be at war all the time.

A court attendant enters and announces in a loud voice.

Court Attendant   His Excellency and Majesty, our Benefactor the Most High God.

A door covered in green padding is swung open and the Most High God enters followed by officials of his court, soldiers, angels, and representatives of the press, and television. All those present stand up, then bow low with humility. He settles on his throne and Master Radwan begins the proceedings as soon as the court officials, the courtesans, and the media representatives have left the room.

Master Radwan   This is a closed summit meeting convened by our Most High God with the aim of permitting an exchange between him and his benevolent emissaries concerning problems affecting the universe. Your

Excellencies attended the plenary meeting and are now conversant with the problems which face us today and which must be solved without delay if we are to preserve the highest of all thrones. We cannot let any harm come to it as long as we continue to exist. We are the protectors of this throne, is that not so, Your Excellencies?

Everybody nods in agreement. Master Radwan drinks some water from a silver vessel and resumes what he was saying.

Master Radwan   Perhaps the most important thing that has occurred today has been Satan's resignation. I tried to make him withdraw it and resume his whispering into people's ears, but he refused to budge and now we have no alternative, Your Excellencies, but to chose one of you to assume the role of Satan. Otherwise, we will find ourselves in a very difficult situation. No one can imagine a world without Satan. Please tell me what you think we should do.

There is complete silence. Nobody makes a move. They all turn and look at one another hesitantly. An atmosphere of anxiety and fear reigns.

Master Radwan   If no one volunteers our Lord and Benefactor will be obliged to choose someone from amongst you. So what do you have to say?

Prophet Abraham   It is Allah's right to choose whomever he wants and we have no other alternative than to obey and be patient. I am an old man and my voice is ugly. Satan should be an attractive youth who can seduce people. Where seducing is concerned, I am absolutely useless.

Prophet Moses   I also am old and ugly. People will be repelled by me if I assume the role of Satan. That way, whether we have a Satan or not, will not make any difference.

Prophet Muhammad   I, too, won't serve your purpose, Master Radwan. My youth is no more and I am incapable of whispering into people's ears. My voice is also too powerful.

All eyes turn towards Jesus, the handsome young man.

Master Radwan Will you accept this post, Lord Jesus, for the sake of your Father?

Jesus Christ Master Radwan, for the sake of my Father I was crucified and tortured and it would not be just for that to happen again. Master Radwan, why don't you play the role of Satan? You have lived all your days in the plenitude and comfort of Paradise, and it's only just that you should know some pain and suffering such as we have experienced.

All the prophets and emissaries present in the meeting immediately express their approval of this suggestion, sigh relief and clamor in unison: A very good idea. We all agree.

Master Radwan's face expresses fear and horror. He turns towards the Most High God as though looking to him for rescue.

The Most High God Radwan is my right hand and I cannot do without him. Anyhow, we will postpone this question of Satan's post until we have dealt with the other items. Go ahead, Master Radwan.

Master Radwan (*reading from a piece of paper*) The second item is the election of the new prophet who will be sent to set what is happening in the world right. Prophet Muhammad has asked the Most High God to send him once more with the task of making people go back to the right path. However, our Highest of all Lords considers it necessary to consult all of you on this matter. All of you are his prophets and emissaries, whom he sees as equal, and in whom he has full confidence. Therefore, he wishes you to be free in choosing who will be the new prophet amongst you.

There is total silence. Each one of those present is in deep thought. No one says anything. After some time, Prophet Abraham's voice can be heard speaking slowly.

Prophet Abraham Since no one has volunteered, in my capacity as the eldest of those present and the father of all prophets, I propose Prophet Moses. He is the eldest prophet after me, the most experienced and the most wise. These qualities are necessary in the new prophet.

Master Radwan Excellencies, what do you think of this proposal?

Prophet Muhammad   You will excuse me, Prophet Abraham, but I do not agree. Prophet Moses will support his people, the sons of Israel, whereas the biggest problem in the world today is Israel. Therefore, the new prophet cannot be one of the sons of Israel. Instead of him, I propose Jesus Christ.

Master Radwan   What do you think, Jesus Christ?

Jesus Christ   First of all I wish to thank Prophet Muhammad for selecting me, but I fear that if I go back to that world my fate will be crucifixion and torture once again.

Jesus Christ looks round as though searching for someone.

Jesus Christ   Your Excellencies, have you not noticed that all those present are men? There is not a single woman amongst us. What will I have to say to the feminist women in the world of today when I go back to them? I beg of you, leave me out when you think of someone to play this role!

Prophet Muhammad   There are women well fitted to be prophets including my first wife, Mistress Khadijah. She was the first one to adopt Islam and when Gabriel descended on me in the cave of Har'a, I went back to her trembling in fear and asked her to wrap me up warmly. I did not know what to do. She was the one who gave me courage and said to me "you are the emissary of Allah." Were it not for her I would never have stood firmly on my feet and Islam would not have arisen.

Jesus Christ   And my mother, Virgin Mary, the most virtuous of women as described in the Qur'an, Brother Muhammad. God chose her among all women, elevated her above them and consecrated a whole "soura" to her in the Qur'an, named the "Soura of Mariam." However, Brother Muhammad, the name of your lady, Khadijah, was never once mentioned. The only woman mentioned in the Qur'an is my mother Mary. What do you think of that, Brother Muhammad?

Prophet Muhammad   I think you are right, Brother Jesus. People often asked me why Mistress Khadijah's name was never mentioned in the Qur'an and I said to them that perhaps Allah, in his wisdom, had a reason for that which human beings were unable to see.

Prophet Abraham   Virgin Mary, daughter of Haroun, is most virtuous, but can we elect her in her absence, Master Radwan? Why don't you ask her and others from amongst the great women in history to attend? Perhaps God can set things right in the universe by sending a woman prophet after all we men have failed.

Master Radwan consults with the Most High God in whispers. The whispers go on for some time before Master Radwan rings a bell and sends soldiers to call in the Virgin Mary and other women, including Bint Allah. They take a back seat. After a short while Eve comes in with other women well known in history, including the ancient goddesses Maat, and Isis, Queen Nefertiti, and Cleopatra, and Rabia al-Adaweya, a founder of the Sufi sect.

Master Radwan   (*addressing the women*) The Most High God has ordered that some virtuous women attend this summit meeting. God Almighty said in his three Holy Books that he has created the human beings from one self, male and female, that no human being is considered better than another except by his or her degree of righteousness and good deeds. There are many women in history who are famous for their righteousness and good deeds, including Mary the mother of Jesus, Mistress Khadijah the wife of Prophet Muhammad, and the mother of Prophet Moses who saved him from Pharaoh, Mistress Hagir who saved the life of her son Ishmael, and many other mothers and wives who showed courage and sacrificed their lives to raise high the word of truth. The Most High God has given orders that you be present in order to participate in deciding who should be the new prophet delegated to shoulder the task of setting things right in the world now drowning in blood, in wars and in injustices. I just received a fax informing me that two hundred thousand children died of hunger as they fled from the war in Zaire, Rwanda, and Burundi, and that seventy youths and children were killed during an attack on unarmed Palestinian people. In addition, the big nuclear powers wish to force nuclear disarmament on all other countries of the world with the exception of Israel.

The Most High God is extremely angry with the rulers of the world. They have sown corruption everywhere, and have applied double standards all the time. The Almighty has therefore decided to send down a new prophet in order that they be reminded of his Word and be guided by him to the straight and narrow path. He might decide to send a woman prophet for there is no reason why all prophets should be men. We, therefore, wish you to express your opinion in this matter and propose a candidate to accomplish this role.

Eve raises her hand.

Master Radwan   Please go ahead, Mistress Eve.

Eve   Master Radwan, I wonder why my name does not appear among the women who played a role in history. Why are you following in the steps of your Most High Lord by denying that I was the first to lead the human race to knowledge and not to death as he says in his Books. He mentioned my name in his first book, the Torah, but accused me of original sin. Then, he left out my name completely from his third book, the Qur'an. He confined himself to describing me as the wife of Adam, but made him share the responsibility for original sin with me when he said, "And we said to Adam dwell you and your wife in Paradise and eat of its good things you desire, but do not approach the tree and so become one of the unjust, but Satan led them astray, and caused them to be deprived of what they had." Here your Most High God speaks of them in the dual form as a proof that both of them, both Adam and his wife, committed a sin. Yet he forgives only Adam when he says: "He heard words from Adam and forgave him for He is the Compassionate and the All Forgiving." No doubt your Most High God possesses an unparalleled knowledge of grammar related to the Arabic language and so he is precise in expressing what he wants to say. Thus I, Eve, became the sinful in the eyes of all people who believe in Your Most High God and in his Books, whereas Adam came out innocent, although he was corrupt and although the angels protested against his being made the representative of your Most High God on earth and said, "Do you appoint him who will sow corruption and shed blood?", according to what is mentioned in the Qur'an. Do you know how your Most High God answered the angels? He said, "I know what you do not know;" considered himself all knowledgeable and me an ignoramus with no knowledge at all. Yet, I possess the most basic and most important of all knowledge, knowledge which springs from my experience in life. Knowledge, Master Radwan, comes only from experience in a particular place and at a particular moment. Your Most High God exists outside of time and place, so where can his knowledge come from?! Knowledge, Master Radwan, springs from the senses and the mind during a lived experience.

Master Radwan   This is a pure nonsense, Mistress Eve. How can knowledge come from the senses and the mind? The Most High God is the source of all knowledge. We gain knowledge not from our experiences, but from the Almighty All-Sacred God. He is the one who bestows knowledge upon us not experience or practice. We can only know what God wishes us to know, Mistress Eve. God the Almighty, the All-High teaches us to "say we will only have what Allah has ordained for us. Allah guides whom He wishes and leads astray whomsoever He wishes."

Prophet Muhammad   True, Master Radwan, but Allah also said in the Holy Qur'an, "And Allah brought you out of your mothers' bellies knowing nothing and gave you hearing, and sight and feelings in order that you be grateful." We are born, Master Radwan, with minds that are a white page, not knowing anything. Then we learn and gain knowledge through hearing, seeing, and feeling. Feelings mean the heart, which is what the heart feels.

Eve   What you said means that we gain knowledge through our senses, through what we see, and hear, and live. This contradicts the verse quoted from the Qur'an which says, "Allah guides whomever he wishes to guide, and leads astray whomever He wishes to lead astray." It means that only Allah possesses knowledge, gives it to whomever he wants, and deprives whomever he decides to deprive from it. In other words, people are born with their fate, their destiny already decided, and human beings have no choice, can gain no knowledge from the realities of their life through their senses. Everything is fixed, already known, written down irrespective of the experiences they live through. If God has imposed on human beings either to advance on the right path or to go astray they cannot be responsible for what they do, and God alone is to be held responsible, to be held accountable, because human beings, if they follow the right path or go astray, do not choose. Everything is decided for them, imposed on them by God. To be obliged to do something, to have no choice means one is freed of responsibility if one does it. That is a principle of justice, is it not, Master Radwan? Is it not, your Excellencies, men and women, here present in this gathering?

Prophet Abraham   Yes, Mistress Eve, to oblige, to impose on people frees them from responsibility. Similarly, human beings are responsible for their actions, but not for the actions of others. I questioned the Most High God more than once when he ordered me to burn down a whole city and kill everyone in it because ten or twenty, at most, of its inhabitants, had gone astray.

Prophet Muhammad   That is exactly what Allah mentions in the Qur'an when he says, "Do not blame one for what the other does. Each one according to his doings."

Prophet Abraham   Yes, Prophet Muhammad, but Allah the Almighty, the Sacred also said, "I cannot do either good or bad to myself." That means I have no power to do anything good or bad to myself, let alone to others. There is another verse in the Qur'an, Prophet Muhammad, which says, "If something bad happens to you it will have come from you, and if it is something good it will have come from Allah." The verses of the Qur'an contradict one another, say one thing and then refute it, say one thing and then the opposite, so that we never know the truth.

Prophet Muhammad   To understand these verses, we must put them in their context. Every verse was born in a different situation. For example, Allah commanded me to wage war in order to raise his Word high up. Fight against those who do not believe in Allah and his Prophet. In other situations he would order me to refrain from killing and tell me to negotiate and settle things peacefully. If they lean towards peace, be ready to do the same. We have to know the place and the time of each verse in order to understand it and know why it was sent down.

Jesus Christ But do you not believe that I was crucified, Prophet Muhammad? Allah in the Qur'an says, "And they did not kill him or crucify him. They just imagined he was." In Christianity we believe in God, in the Son of God, and in the Holy Ghost. We believe in three Gods in one, not just one indivisible God. If each human being is only responsible for what he does and not for what others do, why does God punish all of us for Eve's sin?

Eve And what sin did I commit?! According to what the Most High God says in his heavenly Books, I had only two paths between which to choose. The first path was not to eat from the tree and live eternally in ignorance. The second path was to eat from the tree and gain knowledge, but be deprived of remaining eternal. I preferred knowledge with a finite existence to an eternal life spent in ignorance.

Master Radwan Not to be eternal means that death becomes your fate. Knowledge means to couple with Adam and have children, is that not so, Mistress Eve?

Eve Yes, that is true, but what is wrong with having sex, being pregnant, and giving birth, Master Radwan? Your Most High God has said to us humans: multiply and bear children. How was that to happen if I and my husband had not eaten from the tree and known the meaning of sex together? We were obliged to choose between obeying God and between practicing sex and having children. Obedience to God meant we would have had no offspring, and that would have meant an end to human beings. To disobey him also meant death. Both obedience and disobedience therefore led to death. The real choice, therefore, was between death without having sex or offspring and between death after having sex and bearing children, and this is what we chose because it meant life would continue on earth, and that human beings would not become extinct, Master Radwan. Thus, the human race is indebted to me because I disobeyed God and had more courage, and was more aware than my husband, Adam. Nevertheless, your Most High God chose to put the blame on me, to punish me cruelly by making my husband rule over me, although I was more reasonable and wiser than he was. In fact, he punished all the daughters of Eve by making men responsible for women, by making them rule over them in the family and the state.

Master Radwan   The state, like the family, is a collective of people and it must have a single leader to take decisions when they differ. It was inevitable that Adam should be made the leader, Mistress Eve, since he obeyed God and understood his orders better than you did. You were more rebellious and disobeyed him, so he decided to impose obedience to your husband on you. Thus, if you obey your husband, you will be obeying the Most High God.

Eve   You mean that your Most High God was unable to force obedience on me directly and so decided to do it through my husband. After that he imposed the "law of obedience" on all the women in the world. He appointed man as trustee, as a patron over woman, over her morals, her humor, her virginity, her marital fidelity. He accorded her husband the authority to supervise her behavior and her faithfulness to him, but deprived her of any authority or rights. He legitimized marital infidelity for men by allowing them to marry more than one woman or have slaves or concubines. And all this happened because I am Eve, the sinful, yet who committed no sin and is the main reason why humanity exists.

There is silence in court. The heads of the men are bent in thought.

Master Radwan   The main reason why humanity has continued to exist is due to the will of the Most High and Most Sacred of all gods. If he had so wished, the human race would have perished completely, but he desired it to exist, and used Adam and Eve as his instruments, used them to fulfill his will. This is his absolute right over us, his slaves; for it was he who created us and we should worship and obey him because he is more knowledgeable than we are. The Most High God knows that men are more obedient to him than women. That is why he speaks to men since this is easier than having to address both sexes. In addition, imposing one husband only on women permits the father to know his offspring so that his descendants are not confused with those of others. When there is more than one wife, this confusion cannot exist because the father is known.

Bint Allah   That is the case when the line of descent is patrilinear. If it is matrilineal, there is no problem. Nowadays there are many countries that allow children to be affiliated with their mothers or to both the father and the mother. To ignore the name of the mother is to persist in ignoring the rights of women and her role in history. In the matriarchal societies, which preceded the reign of a single male God, children were affiliated to the mother. At that time there were female goddesses, like Maat the goddess of Justice, and Isis the goddess of Knowledge. That is why there were women who were called "al-Arrafa" (she who knows the fortune teller). Ancient kings and emperors used to have recourse to them to read the future. In North Africa, the goddess of the future was called "Dihar," but her name is no longer mentioned in history. The same thing happened to many women of wisdom in the Middle Ages, often branded as witches and sorcerers who were burnt to death because they were said to have relations with Satan or to have disobeyed the church.

Among the Arab women is Zarka'a al-Yamame, an "Arrafa" who could see what others failed to perceive, as well as Afira'a and al-Zabra'a from the tribe of Beni Ri'am. Al-Zabra'a was able to warn her tribe of impending attacks from her enemies and recited poetry, the language of which was just as miraculous as that of the Qur'an. Belkis, the Queen of Sheba, was able to prophesy that the dam of Ma'areb would collapse. Master Radwan, history was turned upside down since your Most High God ascended to the throne. He killed the mother of mothers and named her the Great Adulteress of Babel. The Arrafa (woman of knowledge), the goddess of knowledge, became an evil sinner and ignorant woman, "without mind or faith." She was not allowed to speak, for her voice was considered to be sacrilegious, her face was not to be shown in countries like Saudi Arabia, her vote not to be cast, her candidature to elections refused in countries like Kuwait, her passport not to be renewed except with her husband's permission in countries like Egypt. As for women in America and Europe, in the West, Master Radwan, they are still under the domination of their husbands. They receive a lesser wage for the same work as men. The majority of women in the world, in the East or West, in North and South suffer poverty, to a degree which has led the United Nations to coin a new term "feminization of poverty." There is a well-known man of religion in Egypt called Sheikh Sha'arawi who considers himself the representative of your Most High God on earth. Women actresses and dancers have recoursed to him in order to repent before God, since for a woman's voice to be heard singing or for her to appear on the stage or on a television or film screen is sacrilegious. He even preaches the banning of music and says that it comes from Satan. This Sheikh, Master Radwan, has also declared that the Most High God disallows the transplantation of human organs like the kidney. His exact words were: "The transportation of kidneys or washing of the kidneys to treat renal failure delays the encounter of a human being with his God and they are therefore unholy."

Prophet Muhammad What this Sheikh is saying is just nonsense. Allah does not tell us to die, but to live. The verses of the Qur'an encourage us to live. If the Muslims follow what this Sheikh is saying about life and death, what he described as delaying the encounter of a human being with his God, they would disappear off the face the earth. In the world of today new discoveries follow one after the other in the fields of science and medicine. They help the human being to resist disease and death, to live. This does not mean opposing the will of Allah since all this is a result of his powers, of what he decides. Allah gave us a mind to use in making life better, more just, more beautiful. I have a saying, Master Radwan, which goes as follows: Do for your world as though you will live forever, and do for the afterworld as though you will die tomorrow.

Silence reigns in the room. Voices are heard coming from outside. People are shouting slogans in a demonstration. The Sudanese people are out in the streets demonstrating against their government.

They shout in unison: Enough of religion. We need bread. Enough of religion. We need Tamween.

Bint Allah Those are the voices of women, children, and men asking for bread instead of verses from the Divine Books. Yesterday a Sudanese father killed his four children. In the inquest he said, "It was an order from Allah." The man's name was Khamees Almaskeen (Thursday the Miserable). After committing his crime he told the police that he had followed an order sent down from heaven. The children's ages ranged between four and nine years. He smashed their heads with a heavy butcher's knife. An Egyptian mother named Sahar Mahmoud Ahmed killed her only child, a one-year-old girl called Yasmine Mostapha Hassan. She suffocated her with a pillow and then carried her body to the police station. There she said she killed her to save her from a life of poverty, so that she would be sent to Paradise, an innocent child who had not committed any sin. Four women were killed in the midst of a crowd as they struggled for a share in the flour which was being distributed in the town of Kafr al-Dawaar. A man and his wife threw their child into the streets because the wife had become pregnant before they were officially married. They killed their baby fearing the scandal they would face. Girls and young women are killed to save the honor of the family; children are punished if the name of the father is not known. They are called "illegitimate" and are deprived of all human rights. Two million illegitimate children live on the streets in Cairo of Egypt. The name of the mother has no honor; if a child carries the name of his mother he is considered illegitimate by the state and divine law in Egypt and many other countries. Wives often commit suicide because their husbands marry another woman or are unfaithful to them. Men often divorce their wives for the flimsiest of reasons because there are no legal restrictions to hold them back. Fathers sell their young daughters for a price to old men with money under the guise of marriage. Women are beaten up by their men who refer to a verse in the Qur'an which says, "Beat them and abandon the marital bed." All these tragedies found are supported by the rulings of "Sharia" (religious jurisprudence).

Prophet Muhammad The Sharia, my child, has nothing to do with what you describe. Allah will bring those who are guilty of such actions to account on the Day of Judgment. They will be punished severely.

Prophet Abraham Prophet Muhammad, they should be punished on earth and not in the hereafter. All these crimes happen here on earth and accountability should be made immediate and not postponed until after death. To postpone punishment is to delay justice. Delayed justice is, itself, an injustice. A delay of justice for one day is equivalent to an injustice which lasts one year.

Master Radwan Don't you believe in the hereafter and in the Day of

Judgment?! You, the father of all prophets, the father of the monotheistic message, the first to have known monotheism in human history?!!

Prophet Abraham   The Torah does not speak of one God, but of "Alouheem" of a group or number of gods. Monotheism started late in Ancient Egypt, during the reign of Ekhnatoun and Nefertiti. The ancient Egyptians had many gods, including provincial gods, city gods, gods of the capital or main cities, state gods, gods for the various forces of nature, gods for the kings, and gods for the people. The conception of accountability of a day of judgment after death, of the hereafter, was familiar to the ancient Egyptians centuries before the Torah was known. The truth of the matter is that the doctrine of judgment and accountability was initiated by women in ancient Egypt. They initiated the first conceptions of justice. Goddess of Justice, Maat, arose at that time, and women were the first of all beings in whom human conscience came into existence.

Goddess Maat   In ancient Egypt people in the courts of justice used to say to their hearts, "O heart, inherited from my mother, heart with which I was born and with which I have lived, do not bear witness against me in front of my mother, for I have not lied, nor stolen, nor killed."

Goddess Isis   Our mother of mothers, Nut, raised us in the respect of justice. When I succeeded her on the throne, she told me that the sacred standing which gods occupy does not arise from their being the objects of people's worship, but from the degree of justice with which they rule, that the long journey in search of gods ends with a mirror in which the human being sees himself or herself to be just. The male gods in Egypt became gods of state, involved in war and fighting, whereas women were busy with agriculture and with ensuring that justice prevailed among people. The gods of state kept changing with the ruling system, starting with Hor, then Miftah in the ancient kingdom. They were followed by Atoun Ra'a, then Ameen or Amoun who united with Atoun Ra'a in the Middle Kingdom. The ruling god was a main pillar in a triple-structured family composed of the father, the mother, and the son or daughter. Gods were like human beings; they married and had children. Then, the triple structure developed into a nine-pillar family. The biggest and most powerful groups were composed of nine gods. In ancient Greece the gods of Olympia were counted by the hundreds. The multiplicity of gods is not a sign of backwardness, neither does monotheism mean progress. In the Christian West people believe in God the Father, Jesus the son, and the Holy Ghost, that is three gods, in a triple structure, and they are not more backward than those who believe in one God. The multiplicity of gods in the civilization of Egypt and other agricultural river civilizations, like that of Iraq, was progressive but desert environments tend towards unification, towards one God. It is natural to the Bedouin for him to realize the value of his sheep as he watches it grazing, or of the moon in the silent desert nights. He is led to compare between the horns of his sheep and the two ends of the crescent. Thus, the sheep becomes a moon in a single system. During the time of Nefertiti and Ekhnatoun the concept of monotheism lasted only seventeen years and was imposed during that period by force, by the sword, by massacres, and by torture. In the Qur'an the Most High God says: "The punishment of those who fight against Allah and His Prophet, who sow corruption on earth is death, or crucifixion, or cross amputation of their arms and legs, or to live in the world as wandering exiles."

Prophet Muhammad   That is the fate of those that sow corruption over the land, not of the righteous who seek justice and do good.

Prophet Abraham   True, Prophet Muhammad, but the problem is who decides what is good and what is evil. Adam was corrupt, sowed corruption in the land and shed blood, and yet he became God's representative on earth.

Prophet Muhammad   It is Allah who decides who of us is corrupt and who is righteous.

Prophet Abraham   But God does not live amongst people on earth. It is the rulers who judge them, who apply that verse. For example, the King of Saudi Arabia cuts off the head of youths who oppose him and then reads the verse you quoted from the Qur'an.

Prophet Muhammad   But there are young people who carry the Qur'an and revolt against their rulers in defense of justice and freedom.

Prophet Abraham   Thus, it is that the Book of God can be used to defend what is just and right and to defend injustice and evil.

Bint Allah   That is why there is no such thing as the absolute truth in the word of God. The truth of Allah's words is always relative depending on the power which has recourse to it. In some countries women have started to cooperate with one another and to represent a new force that interprets the Torah, or the Bible, or the Qur'an in a way which favors their liberation, rather than maintain their slavery. For example, they no longer address God as masculine in the language they use. Every religion refers to God as being masculine and even if this is only a matter of language it inevitably places women in an inferior position compared to men. English, French, Hebrew, and Arabic are all masculine languages which have dropped women from consideration. This is not only the case with language but with all signs and symbols related to religion. All of them are inimical to women, but also to the poor. If the heavenly God is male, then rulers on earth must also be male, for God is a model for human beings. If God's words contradict one another, then contradictory words and behavior or dualism become characteristic of human beings. If God's words are lacking in their logic, are irrational, then the language of people will have the same characteristics.

Master Radwan   The word of God, young girl, is above all logic, superior to all reason, yet neither against reason nor against logic.

Bint Allah   That is also contradictory, Master Radwan. How can words be logical and at the same time be beyond all reason and all logic?

Master Radwan   You are saying very dangerous things against our Almighty and Most Sacred of all Gods. What is your name?

Bint Allah   My name is Bint Allah.

Master Radwan   (*in fear*) God help me. We have never heard of that name before. Your name is heresy.

Jesus Christ   Why, Master Radwan? If there is a son of God, why shouldn't there be a daughter of God?

Prophet Moses   God said in the Torah that he has sons only, but no daughters.

Prophet Abraham   (*laughing*) Prophet Moses, that kind of talk is out of date. It must be quoted in its context, related to place and time, otherwise in our days it will sound ridiculous.

Eve   In ancient times, Adam and I gave birth to many girls and boys. The problem always was that the corrupt son became God's representative on earth. Satan was one of my sons but he was righteous and sought for the truth and for knowledge, the way I did. He became a danger to the greatest of all rulers on earth and challenged his authority. It is the struggle over power which caused lots of blood to flow throughout history.

Bint Allah   Many were the women who were killed. First and foremost was the mother of all mothers in the city of Babel. Amongst them also was Manat. She was the goddess of death and her mother the goddess Sikhmet, who lived in Egypt. Also, the goddess al-Ozza, the word of al-Ozza meaning pride and power. She was a black woman and was poor with thick coarse hair and a strong will. Khalid ibn al-Waleed struck her with his sword and split her head in two, killed her supporters, and cut down her tree. She was the goddess in whom the Prophet Muhammad believed when he still held to the faith of his tribe. He gave her the sheep Afra'a as an offering. At that time, she had a square white stone in the town of al-Tarif which people worshipped, but Manat had a black stone which is considered sacred by Arabs. Queen Hatshepsut ruled in Ancient Egypt for over twenty years. Her husband was Amenophis II. The Pharaoh who fought against Moses was named Meneftah and his mummy is to be found today in the hall of the Egyptian Museum where lay all the royal mummies, which contradicts what is mentioned in the Divine Book about him.

Prophet Muhammad   No, young lady. Allah in the Holy Qur'an said that when Pharoah was defeated by the armies of Moses and was drowning, he said to Allah, "I believe that there is no God other than the one in whom the children of Israel believe and I now declare my submission to Him." But Allah answered him saying, "Now that you disobeyed me in the past,

and committed aggression against me, I do put you aside with your body
so that you serve as an example to others who came after you." There might
be contradictions in the Torah and the Bible, and may be many distortions
have crept into them, but the Qur'an is the exact word of Allah whom no
one has ever changed.

Prophet Abraham　No, Prophet Muhammad, the three Holy Books
have been the object of distortions because they were transmitted by
human beings, who narrated them and this led inevitably to changes in
the words and the meaning. To make sure of accuracy and truthfulness,
it was necessary that the word of God be transmitted directly to people
without going through prophets, interpreters, or translators. For example,
Pharaoh did not speak Arabic. Yet his words in the Qur'an are spoken in
the Arabic language, so how is that possible? Part of the meaning must be
lost during translation since we cannot separate between the letters and
their meaning. The words of God should have reached people directly, in
their local languages, without the need for translations, interpreters or even
prophet. For example, when God used to speak to me I didn't always absorb
everything to the letter. I used to transmit what he said to me according
to my understanding. As a result, the words of God always change when
they reach people through human beings. The Torah was transmitted in
Hebrew, then it was translated into Greek during the reign of Ptolemy
Bartholomew Philadelphus. In the year 285 BC Ptolemy Bartholomew
sent to the High Priest Elazar asking for a copy and seventy-two translators. Elazar responded to this quest. This delegation, when it arrived, was
joined by Demetrius, one of Barthalomew's aids. They went off to an isolated island, completed their task in seventy-two days and were awarded
precious gifts by the King. Each translator was made to seclude himself
in a separate room. They translated one word after the other, sometimes
working in twos helped by a clerk. The translation was thus completed at
the request of an Egyptian emperor for the benefit of the royal library in
Alexandria. And Master, of course you know that there are many terms
in Arabic without an equivalent in Greek. In addition, no translator can
rid himself completely of his own particular way of understanding a text.
For example, the prophet Shoueib once said, "Here we have a virgin, who

gives birth," but a translator named Shaaban al-Sheikh rendered it as "Here we have a girl who gives birth," whereas there is a big difference between the words "virgin" and "girl." There are many phrases and meanings which changed during the translation of the original Hebrew text into the version produced by the seventy-two translators. So here is a question, Master. Why did Bartholomew Philadelphus spend all that money and give away all those gifts to translate the Torah and distribute it to his people?! Does anyone of you know what the emperor used to do to anyone who disobeyed him? He used to burn him alive or slaughter him or crucify him. His ideal model was the Most High God and the proof he needed to explain his acts was in the Torah.

Master Radwan   What's happened to you, Prophet Abraham? Have you lost your faith in the highest of gods? ·

Prophet Abraham   No, Master Radwan, but I want him to be our ideal example where truth, justice, and compassion are concerned. I believe that his three Books are no longer suitable, that we need a fourth book in which he can correct what is wrong with the previous ones, and which he can send down directly without recourse to an intermediary, to a prophet, or an interpreter, or a translator. That way we will have his original words, and their meaning will be clear and understandable to all the different peoples who have their own language or their own dialect. All prophets, and I am foremost among them, all those who explained or interpreted the sacred books are guilty of submitting to the influence of emperors and kings and rulers, who were corrupt starting with the emperor Philadelphus down to King Fahd and Benjamin Netanyahu in Israel and including the rulers who massacred people in Rwanda, Zaire, South Africa, North Africa, Asia, Europe, North and South America and Australia, as well as those who occupied the capital of Afghanistan a few days ago and who in the name of God prevented women from going to schools or finding work.

Prophet Muhammad   No, Prophet Abraham, people like that have nothing to do with Allah.

Prophet Abraham   Who are the people, then, who have to do with Allah?

Prophet Muhammad   We, the prophets, came close to Allah.

Prophet Abraham   What difference is there between us and ordinary people?

Prophet Muhammad   The will of God dwells in us.

Bint Allah   Why should the will of God not be distributed in a just manner to all people?

At this point Rabia al-Adaweya raises her hand.

Rabia al-Adaweya   Every creature, Excellencies, bears witness to the existence of Allah and no one is alone a proof of his existence. It is through my deep love for him that I discovered that he exists in me. We cannot discover our real selves except if we no longer concentrate on the self. Getting rid of our ego, destroying it, is a necessary condition, without which we cannot love Allah and be one with him. Allah is the supreme power who makes it possible for us to be rid of ourselves, of our ego. We abolish the self, we let it perish in order to become a part of a much broader humane self, freed of our narrow egotistic self. We become united with the other, with Allah, with nature and people and with the history of humanity. Excellencies, I found myself in Allah. I struggled for a long time, traveled all over searching for Allah. My efforts, my extensive travels ended with the mirror in which I saw myself. I reached the pinnacle of happiness when I found myself in Allah. But before that could happen, I had to lose myself in the other, in him. Belief in Allah is love, love of Allah, of nature, of people, of beauty. It is a readiness to die, to lose the self for love, to let it perish in the other. To die for that love is not death, but a return to real life, where we discover our real self.

Isis   What you have said, Mistress Rabia, is beautiful and we consider you the mother of Sufi philosophy. But history as it was written has neglected you because you did not leave any written books behind you, unlike ibn Arabi, who was adopted by some of the rulers. They studied his teaching and put them in print. This also happened with Prophet Abraham and Prophet Muhammad. Powerful caliphs adopted their teachings, collected them, and had them printed. Were it not for that they would have vanished from history. Were it not for the three Books, the Torah, the Bible, and the Qur'an, which are reprinted by kings and rulers in millions of copies, people would have known nothing about Abraham, or Moses, or Jesus Christ, or Muhammad. Nor would they have known anything about the heavenly God who was chosen by Abraham from among the group of gods called "Alouheem," the same heavenly God who later on was worshipped by Moses, then Muhammad. The name "Allah" is a modified Arabic version of the name al-Laah, which originally was al-Lat written with a "t" at the end. Al-Lat was the female goddess who was worshipped in the Arab peninsula together with the goddesses Manat and al-Ozza.

There arose a struggle over land and money between the tribes which worshipped the goddesses and other tribes which started to worship male gods, such as the god Baal and the god Yahua and the god al-Lah as well as other gods. The struggle was over land and money but it was carried on in the name of the goddesses and gods just as happened in ancient Egypt. In Egypt, people worshipped Isis, the goddess of knowledge of wisdom and of the movement of ships. Isis says, "I am the one who used to guide sailors and ships in the big sea. I taught men and women how to grow wheat and barley. My mother, Nut, taught me how to bury the seeds, cover them with earth, and irrigate them with the water of the Nile, then wait until the green shoots began to show. When my mother waited for them to appear, she used to follow the movement of the sun with wonder and that of the moon at night." That is how she discovered time and sun clock. She divided up time according to the movements of the sun and the moon. She calculated the passage of day by lines on the earth, which she drew in the form of numbers the way she had seen her mother, Nut, do. She calculated the length of the night, then the day and night together, then the seven days which make up the week, and then the year which she found was made up of three hundred and sixty-five days. We women, Mistress Rabia, were the first ones who developed knowledge. We discovered agriculture, astronomy, arithmetic, algebra, geometry, music, poetry. We were the first to write down letters and numbers, taught people the names of the stars, and planets, discovered and calculated the leap year. Mothers taught their daughters and their granddaughters and so knowledge was handed down from generation to generation. They initiated astrology then astronomy, built towers in Upper Egypt to follow the movements of stars and planets in space. The most important were two towers in Sekouf in the temple of Dandara, and two close to the city of Esna. The temple of Dandara is four thousand years old and that of Esna is seven thousand years old.

Master Radwan   What are these things you are saying? What you have told us is all wrong. It was God who taught Adam the names of things including the names of the stars.

Bint Allah   No, Master Radwan, what our grandmother Isis has been telling us is true. It was published in Cairo by a newspaper called *Monitor* during the month of August 1800. It caused uproar in Europe and the Church protested because it believes that human life began as registered in the Holy Bible.

Prophet Abraham   There are three Bibles: a Hebrew Bible, a Sumerian Bible, and the one translated into Greek. Each one gives a different figure for the age of the human species varying from 2023 years to 2324 years to 3329 years.

Bint Allah   In the year 1793, Dubois began a battle over this question after he made a study of the Egyptian astronomical towers. He said that the Egyptian civilization goes back fifteen thousand years. The Church raised uproar in Europe because this is in contradiction with the Torah. In 1798, Napoleon invaded Egypt. The scientists who went with his expedition visited the four towers of Dandara and Esna in Upper Egypt. In January 1882, the tower of Dandara was stolen and shipped to Marseilles ,then taken to Paris passing through La Lorraine. It was sold to the government of Louis XVIII for the sum of 150,000 francs and put in the Louvre museum. The authorities of the Church heaped curses on it and named it the "mean" black stone, and an "instrument for spreading atheism" and the denial of God. There arose an acute conflict between the authorities of the Church, led by the priest Tesseta, and the archaeologists led by Dubois. Father Tesseta maintained that the towers of Dandara and Esna had been built in the third century before Christ and that, therefore, they did not contradict the word of God in the Torah. This conflict went on from 1793 until 1880 when the authorities of the Church were proven to be wrong by experts from Egypt, France, Germany, and England, including Champollion, who was able to read the papyruses and the letters of the ancient Egyptian hieroglyphic language. The Church was obliged to admit that the historical account written in the Torah was not correct. The archaeologists in Egypt began to forward proof that the first human being to appear on earth was not the Adam mentioned in the Torah, but another Adam who appeared fifty thousand years ago born of another Eve, who most probably was a black African woman.

Rabia al-Adaweya all the while remains standing and looking into the mirror held up in her hand. Her skin is fair, slightly tanned by the sun.

Bint Allah   (*addresses Rabia al-Adaweya*) You say, Mistress Rabia, that your prolonged travels searching for God ended with that mirror in which you see your face. Is that not so?

Rabia al-Adaweya   Yes, Bint Allah. Are you a woman or still a young girl?

Bint Allah   What difference does that make?

Rabia al-Adaweya   A young girl is addressed as Miss. She is still an unmarried virgin. A woman is addressed as Mistress. She is married and no longer a virgin.

Bint Allah   Do you ask men a similar question?

Rabia al-Adaweya   No.

Bint Allah   Why not?

Rabia al-Adaweya   Because virginity is not a part of a man's personality before marriage. Men do not have a hymen.

Bint Allah   Why should the hymen be considered part of my personality, Mistress Rabia?

Rabia al-Adaweya   Because you are a girl.

Bint Allah   Then what about girls who are born without a hymen? Twenty-five percent of all females are born without a hymen. I will tell you my story. My mother gave birth to me in 1975 where we lived in a small village next to the sea. I saw my father kill his mother. He hit her over the head with a shovel which she used to dig into the earth of a piece of land from which she fed him. He ran away from my mother when she gave birth to me. He wanted a son who would inherit his name and his father's name. My mother worked the land, sent me to a school, and then to the university where I studied history. I got a doctorate degree and became a professor. So is my hymen still a part of my personality? Maybe I was born without a hymen or it tore one day when I jumped down the stairs or rode on a bicycle or a horse. Maybe a man violated me when my mother used to leave me in the care of neighbors when I was eight years old, so that she could go off to work in the fields.

Rabia al-Adaweya   God help us. Is there a man who can do that to a child of eight?!

Prophet Abraham   Yes, Mistress Rabia. There are men, even prophets, who marry children who are still eight or even seven years old. Behavior, like language or anything else, changes with time and place. In our days men used to hand over their women to the enemy to save their own lives. I, myself, let my wife share Pharaoh's bed to protect my life. I lied to him, told him she was my sister.

Bint Allah   Thanks for your comment, Prophet Abraham. What you have said is historically correct and is even mentioned in the Torah. I want to ask Mistress Rabia Al-Adaweya a question.

Rabia al-Adaweya   Please go ahead, Professor.

Bint Allah   When you look into the mirror, what do you see?

Rabia al-Adaweya   I see my face.

Bint Allah   Can you describe it to us?

Rabia al-Adaweya (*looking into the mirror*) The face of a woman who is fair, but slightly tanned with long, black hair. [*She laughs*]

Bint Allah You said to us that you see Allah in your face. When you see your face in the mirror, do you see that the face of God resembles your face?

Rabia al-Adaweya Yes, why not? I see Allah in myself!

Master Radwan May God help us. Allah can never have the face of a woman. I pray God the Almighty to forgive us.

Prophet Muhammad God the Almighty, the Most Sacred has neither face, nor tongue, nor body. He, the Most High and Most Sacred, is a spirit without body.

Prophet Abraham How were you able to know that spirit, Prophet Muhammad?

Prophet Muhammad I saw it in my sleep and heard its voice calling to me and saying: Read in the name of your God who created.

Prophet Abraham Was it the voice of God, Prophet Muhammad?

Prophet Muhammad Yes, Father Abraham.

Prophet Abraham How did you know?

Prophet Muhammad Master Gabriel told me that it was the voice of Allah.

Prophet Abraham Was it a man's voice or a woman's voice?

Prophet Muhammad A man's voice.

Prophet Abraham Why do you say it was a man's voice? Why could it not have been a woman's voice? That is where the problem lies, your Excellencies. God came to us in the form of a man with the voice of a man. This picture of him reflects men more than it is a reflection of God. We men imagined him, saw him in our dreams, necessarily as a reflection of our own form, our voices, our morals. We even imagined that there would be fair virgin maidens in Paradise because we wanted to legitimate marital infidelity for ourselves only. We reflected our own reality in what we were imagining. That is why the names of great women have no place in the three Holy Books. The power of women, the power of procreation in the uterus is completely absent from the divine texts. Patrilinear descent erased the names of women. For example, we came to know the names of all Adam's descendants starting with his first son, Sheta, then Anoush until we arrived at Abraham and Noah after 3,389 years. All of them were males. From Abraham to Jesus Christ, throughout the period of 2,200 years that separates between them. Thus, from Adam down to Jesus Christ, over a period of 5,589 years, nothing but males. How can that be?

Master Radwan   Prophet Abraham, we must distinguish between the real events and the literary imaginary events in the Holy Books of Allah the Most High and Most Sacred. In them we find what is real, but we also find symbols, parallels, and imaginary happenings or ambiguity.

Prophet Abraham   Imagination, parallels, ambiguity. It is only human beings who have recourse to ambiguity to hide the truth, because they are lacking or are afraid of the brutality exercised by rulers and so often use symbols. But God is not incapable of communicating the truth, nor does he fear rulers, so why should he have recourse to the use of symbols. Besides, why should all the symbols and the names be masculine? And who is capable of differentiating between the truth, symbols, and what is meant by parallels?

Master Radwan   These are no more than ideas, Prophet Abraham. God alone knows all and is wise.

Prophet Abraham   Ideas become a material force when they dominate people, Master Radwan. They become weapons in the hands of rulers that are used to kill, or laws which condemn to capital punishment or decrees which prevent women from going out to learn or to work. Did you hear the news which was broadcast on October 3, 1996, about how the Taliban forbade women to work or to go to school after they occupied Kabul, the capital of Afghanistan? They did that in the name of the Qur'an. And

Bush, did you not know that on January 16, 1991, he carried the Bible in his hand at the precise moment when he issued orders to drop thousands of bombs on Baghdad? Last month, Netanyahu carried the Torah in his hands when he ordered the massacre of Palestinians in Ramallah. In Saudi Arabia, Kuwait, Somalia, Zaire, Bosnia, Russia, America, and Europe, in all the countries of the world, rulers carry the word of God when they declare war, or kill, or steal, and plunder the resources of other people. Since imperialism has existed it has used the word of God to colonize countries and plunder their resources. Sadat in Egypt used to begin his speeches in the name of Allah, then read out the decisions he had reached in agreement with the World Bank and other institutions which serve the policies of imperialism.

Bint Allah   Yes there are two worlds, a real one which exists on earth and sustains itself by war, by shedding blood, aggression, by old and new colonization, and another unreal world, an imagined world where God lives in the heavens and possesses nothing but ideas. But these ideas are transformed into material power which people on earth control. Thus, there is no separation between reality and imagination, between the heavens and the earth, or between God and human beings. They are all one and God must appear in a human form; otherwise, they cannot know him, cannot imagine that he exists, and cannot love him. Could Mistress Rabia al-Adaweya have such a great love for Allah if he presented himself to you in the form of a snake?

Rabia al-Adaweya   I seek thy protection, O God, from the evil Satan.

Prophet Abraham   The snake was not Satan nor was it the enemy of human beings, so who sowed enmity between them?! Was it not the God of the Torah who insinuated to Adam and Eve that their enemy was the snake, the reptile that led them to the tree of knowledge? In the Qur'an also, Allah told them to descend from Paradise to earth and be enemies to one another. Human beings had lived without enemies, or war, or killings until the God Jehovah came with his earthquakes, his volcanoes, and his wars. He was a God who could not live without fighting against an enemy. If his enemy vanished or died he had to create a new one, imagine another one just as he did by creating Satan. Satan says that without a devil the world system cannot continue. Communism was the devil until the Berlin Wall and the Soviet Union collapsed, so now who is the new enemy?

Prophet Muhammad   The new enemy is now Islam and the Arabs.

Bint Allah   And the poor, as well as the women irrespective of race, sex, or religion. Look how thousands of women and children are being killed in Zaire and Rwanda.

Everyone drops silent and faces look gloomy. At long last the Most High God raises his hand and signals to Master Radwan.

Master Radwan   And now we shall listen to the words of our Most High God, may Allah protect him and save him. (*he realizes his mistake and says*) Pardon me, I mean the words of our Most High God, may he protect himself and maintain himself throughout eternity.

The Most High God   (*in a voice full of sorrow and yearning*) No, Radwan, I do not want to stay on for all eternity. I am tired of being eternal, isolated in the heavens from people, and lonely. When you asked me to attend this summit meeting I came to you in this human form, or else you would have been struck with terror. At first, I wanted to come down to you as a spirit, but a spirit has no form and no existence except in the imagination. How can imagination be transformed into something material or into a force? That is what happens with my Books when they are printed and become laws and principles adopted by religious parties, which are in fact political parties struggling for power, for land, and for money all over the world; whether East or West, North or South. Like you, I was angry at the massacres which led to thousands of victims among the Palestinian people or other peoples in Africa, Asia and elsewhere. I was angered, like you, by the oppression exercised against women in my name or by the plunder of resources and lands also in my name. I was immersed to the hilt in self-worship for over five thousand years, during which I forced you to worship me, although I am no more than an idea in the imagination. After having listened to you men and women, I confess to all of you that I favored men at the expense of women and made the men dominate over women, which was unjust. I also favored Abraham's people and promised to give them land, which belonged to others. I committed many mistakes, and fell into many contradictions, but I also used to revert to my basic human nature, always returned to what is considered good, to justice, equality, compassion, and love. Perhaps for that reason my Books have survived until today. That is why oppressed people and women have found in them weapons with which they can defend their rights. But kings and heads of states have also found in them weapons they can use against women and the poor. But gentlemen and ladies, the human race is moving forwards and very few people go back to the idea of creation as it exists in my Books. Modern science has become the only way to reach true knowledge and my Books are no longer suitable, except to be put in museums or in the hotels of the poor or in the departments of history and religion in schools and universities. That is from an academic point of view. But in the political, social, and cultural spheres of life my Books are the most important sources of knowledge despite the progress in other areas of knowledge. This is dangerous, ladies and gentlemen, this dichotomy between science, politics, and culture. I am primarily responsible for this separation because I separated between the body and the mind or spirit, despite the fact that there is no body without a spirit and no spirit without a body and mind. This idea did not originate with me. I took it over from the mother of the god Ekhnatoun, the goddess Tee. Then he, her son, adopted it from her without referring to its origin and it finally came down to me and I inscribed it in my Torah and omitted to quote him. Thus, the separation between the spirit and the body was not mine at the origin. It was to start with the idea of the Pharaonic male gods in ancient Egypt in their struggle against the mother goddess of wisdom, fertility, and nature. They invented the idea which said that with the birth of every child are born two other children that look like it exactly, but human eyes are unable to see them. Only the god Pharaoh possesses the capacity to do so. The first is called "Ka" and the second "Ba." They are the spirit that enters the child's body until it grows up and dies. At death they leave the body and fly up in the sky in the form of a bird which is the spirit. They also formulated the conception of punishment after death. The spirit is punished at the hands of a goddess who resembles a monster.

She is their enemy, "Nut," who was goddess of the sky, and whose husband was Geb, the god of earth. They also believed in a hereafter after life where people were taken to account for their deeds. In the house of hereafter there was a weighing balance which weighed the good deeds and the bad ones. When a person died a book called the book of the dead was put with him in his tomb. I took all these conceptions over from them and included them in what was written about the hereafter and Paradise in my three Books. The truth, gentlemen and ladies, is that I lived in ancient Egypt and wanted to become its ruler by waging war and killing Pharaoh. I was there at the time of Ramses II, who ruled from 1301 to 1235 BC before the birth of Jesus Christ, whom I made my son. Prophet Moses lived with me in Egypt during the reign of Ramses II, who was called Menfetah, that is, the Pharaoh of the exodus. I fought against him together with Moses and the people of Israel. This was the war in which I was victorious. At that time it so happened that swarms of locusts coming from the desert attacked Egypt. I took the opportunity to say that I had sent the locusts. However, the rich pharaohs and the upper classes all escaped from harm. I used to direct my blow against the poor and the weak, against the women, the children, and the slaves. Circumcision and castration were done only to slaves, never to the pharaohs and the masters. When Egypt submitted to the reign of the Macedonians between 334 and 323 BC after the victory of Alexander the Great, a new capital was established on the shores of the sea and called Alexandria to commemorate his name. The new rulers imposed the Greek language, instead of the Egyptian language; the religion of Isis built on justice, love and freedom was abolished, its priests were killed, and her books and paintings burnt. The Egyptian people were obliged to worship me and my words written in the Greek translation of the Torah. After the death of Alexander, the Byzantine Romans occupied Egypt and Palestine. Palestine was ruled by the Seleucid Syrian Kings in 198 B.C. At all times the translation of my Books, the Torah, the Bible, and the Qur'an was never done except by orders from the ruler.

You said that the rulers fought in my name, but the truth is that I used to wage war in the name of the rulers. I was a Pharaoh who was obliged to flee from Egypt and wanted to establish an empire in the land of Canaan and

Palestine with Moses and the children of Israel. That is why the Torah was formulated in Hebrew. I was addressing my people, the children of Israel, and not the people of Egypt who were under the rule of Ramses II. These are the facts about my history. I erased the name of my mother from history, just as Ekhnatoun did, and I erased the name of Adam's mother also. I usurped the place of the mother of mothers who gave birth to the first child on earth. I established myself as the creator of the universe and said that I created it in six days until science showed all this as untrue. After today's meeting, I cannot go along with this game any longer and things must be put in their proper place. I must admit my mistakes. To admit one's mistakes is better than to go on making them. The time has come for the world to continue its existence, to continue progressing without a God and without a Satan also, without this most harmful separation between the body and the spirit. It is a curse that has tormented human beings for more than five thousand years. It has made the body inferior to the mind and spirit in order that I become the mind and the most high of spirits, in order that the human being with his body be made inferior. Human beings also became divided into men who represent reason and women who are the body. It created an antagonism between man and nature, and between man and other living creatures, including the snake. The most dangerous thing that causes harm to human beings is these divisions. I needed to weaken human beings so that I could become the most powerful of all, so that they would worship me, so that they would fear my hellfire or covet my Paradise. No one ever really loved me because love and fear cannot live together in a heart. I need love, real love without fear of hellfire or hope of Paradise. No one ever gave me this love except Rabia Al-Adaweya. She did not fear hellfire, nor did she covet Paradise. But she fell into the mistake for which I am primarily responsible. She separated between the body and the spirit. She separated between her body and her spirit to the degree that when she looked into the mirror she neither saw her face nor mine, but only the texts and letters written in the Divine Book. She did not see in the mirror. But that was only in her imagination and in the imagination of the people who were her followers. Rabia lived in her imagination. She did not live the real life of women. She sacrificed her body so that she could see me in the mirror. That is not right, for if I created you as men and women, I gave you bodies, minds, and spirits dwelling in the being of the body. If the body is prevented from living, deprived of what it desires, then the mind and the spirit also suffer deprivation. That is why Rabia Al-Adaweya was not happy in her real life. She only knew happiness in her imaginary, illusory life. My conscience feels guilty because this woman gave me so much love and yet in return I only gave her deprivation. In fact, I was a cruel God who tried to compensate for this cruelty with words about compassion and justice. I also was divided myself, since I separated between body and spirit. I denied the existence of my body, and imagined that I was only a spirit in the air. When the crucial moment arrived, when I had to descend to meet you on earth I had no alternative but to face the truth and to put on the body which you now see in front of you. It is the body of a man who says he is not human, the body of a human being who insists he is a God. The time has come for me to be what I really am, to announce my resignation from my position, as a single eternal everlasting God. To be eternal is a curse, not a blessing. Imagine what life can be like when there is no death. I prefer to be a human being that will die, but who enjoys love and life, sex and freedom, and all the pleasures of the world, rather than a God who has life, but is not alive, does not know sex, or love, or freedom, only an eternal emptiness. Love, like freedom, is indivisible. If, in the heavens, there exists neither love nor freedom then it will be the same on earth. If the God of the heavens is a dictator, then rulers on earth themselves cannot be other than dictators.

There is a deep silence. Everybody in the room sits motionless, their expressions gloomy.

The lights go out, and the stage is plunged into darkness.

Loud knocks are heard on the door.

The stage lights up again. It is empty except for Bint Allah. The other characters in the play have all disappeared.

The knocks continue on the door. Then it is broken down and the police enter carrying guns led by their chief, who heads for Bint Allah. He carries a book in his hand.

Chief of Police   You are here and we've been looking for you.

Bint Allah   This is my home, the home of my mother and my grandmother.

Chief of Police   This book, are you the author?

Bint Allah   Yes.

Chief of Police   (*addressing the police*) Put the manacles on her.

Bint Allah   (*in astonishment*) But it's only a play, something imagined.

Chief of Police   (*protesting*) Do you want it to be real also?

SCENE FOUR

Bint Allah is sitting on the dusty ground in chains. We hear the chains clink as she sings in a sad, beautiful voice. She strokes the earth with her palms as she sings.

Bint Allah

This land was her land, and this house was her home.

And the blackberry tree, and the door that opens inwards,
And the oven, the maize cob burner, the comb, the shovel,
And her black robe hanging from a nail.
The straw mat on which her child was born.
She nursed him, taught him to read and write, gave him her mind
I saw him strike her with the shovel and I screamed grandmother.
He buried her in the earth, hid her body,
Then he went along answering to the people that he neither
fathered children, nor had been born of a mother.
That was my father, the greatest of all who are worshipped,
He wanted to kill me also, I his daughter,
He recognizes only his sons as his descendants.

The stage becomes dark except for a faint light. We can hear many voices and a loud noise outside, the noise of women, youth, and children breaking down the door of the prison cell and entering. In the faint light we can see the faces of Isis, Rabia al-Adaweya, Prophets Abraham, Moses, Jesus, and Muhammad, and all the people who disappeared in the previous scene.

Author's Note

God Resigns at the Summit Meeting is based on an actual event that occurred on June 9, 1992 in Cairo, Egypt. Nawal El Saadawi was at home with her husband, Sherif Hatata, the doctor, writer, and activist who spent fourteen years in prison and four years in exile for his political and social beliefs. The couple were awakened after midnight by the sound of familiar knocks at their door. The callers were members of the police, known in Arabic as "visitors of the dawn," who usually appeared unexpectedly to arrest Egyptian men and women who opposed government policies, rather than to arrest Egyptian men and women for suspicion of subversive activities. This practice began during the time of the Pharaohs and has continued until now. Sherif thought that the police had come to arrest him again. It had not occurred to him that this visit was intended for his wife. The police wanted to warn the playwright to take measures to protect herself because her name had appeared on an "assassination list."

Previously, the Egyptian government had attempted to protect El Saadawi by assigning armed guards to her apartment, from December 1988 until December 1990, without explaining the reason for the arrangement and despite her complaints about its ineffectiveness. Rumor had it at the time that the armed protection was necessary because of the controversial theme of *The Fall of the Imam*, a novel written in part when the writer was in prison, two months before the assassination of Anwar El Sadat in 1981. This novel was based on an earlier play in which the imam of the title appeared sometimes in Sadat-like form, considering himself, alternately, as the eternal president on earth or as the powerful

God in the sky. El Sadat considered himself as good as God, blamed his First Minister for all wicked activities, and sacrificed any advocate of opposing views. The play was never published because Egyptian law forbade the personification of prominent figures, including God, his prophets, and El Sadat, on stage. In fact, El Saadawi burned her play to save herself from being sentenced to death for this criminal offense.

During recent years the Egyptian people have become afraid of powerful, unknown groups acting in the name of God through their shootings and bombings. Individuals who have opposed the groups' ideologies have been relentlessly pursued, slandered as infidels, and many have been killed. Such acts have caused El Saadawi, for the first time in her long career, to fear for her life.

The suggestion to move to America came about through Elizabeth, an American student at Duke University, who had visited El Saadawi in Egypt. Elizabeth had studied El Saadawi's work in Arabic classes taught by Dr. Miriam Cook. Alarmed at the sight of the guards and fearing for the writer's safety, Elizabeth contacted Dr. Cook, who arranged for El Saadawi to teach a class as a visiting professor at Duke University.

On October 4, 1996, Dr. Cook and her husband, Dr. Bruce Lawrence, invited her to a student production of *The Fall of the Imam*. It was this performance that inspired and stimulated El Saadawi to revisit the topic she had studied and questioned since she was a young girl. She returned to her apartment on Douglas Street in Durham, North Carolina, and wrote *God Resigns at the Summit Meeting*. She wrote the play from beginning to end in a single, thirteen-hour sitting.

Translated and summarized by Rihab Kassatly Bagnole

Contributors

Rihab Kassatly Bagnole earned a Ph.D. in Interdisciplinary Arts from Ohio University with an emphasis on the visual arts and she has degrees in Fine Arts and Art History, as well as a certificate in Women's Studies. She also has a degree in Business Administration from the University of Damascus in Syria. Bagnole teaches Art History at Ohio University and is also dedicated to women's dance in the Middle East. She has taught and performed Middle Eastern dance at Ohio University and Denison University. She has contributed to *The Green Wood Encyclopedia of World Popular Culture* with entries on "Music in the Middle East and North Africa," "Love, Sex, and Marriage in the Middle East and North Africa," and "Radio and Television in the Middle East and North Africa."

Sherif Hetata is a novelist but graduated with honors as a physician from Cairo University in 1946. He joined the left-wing Democratic Movement for National Liberation and subsequently spent fourteen years in prison (1948–1963). He also spent two years as an exile in Paris (October 1950 to September 1952) after escaping from prison. He has worked as a doctor in hospitals, as a government civil servant in Egypt, as head of a team of experts on Population and Migration for the International Labour Organisation in Asia and Africa, and as a visiting professor at Duke University, the University of Washington, the University of Southern Maine, and the Autonomous University of Barcelona. He is the author of many books in Arabic, including eight novels, two of which have been translated into English, *The Eye with*

An Iron Lid and *The Net*. He is married to novelist and activist Nawal El Saadawi and has translated many of her works into English.

Adele S. Newson-Horst is Professor of English at Missouri State University. She earned a Ph.D. in English from Michigan State University, a M.A. from Eastern Michigan University, and a B.A. from Spelman College where El Saadawi is currently the Distinguished Visiting Professor, Cosby Chair. She is a regular reviewer for *Literature Today*. She has written and/or edited books and articles on Zora Neale Hurston, Gwendolyn Brooks, and Caribbean women writers. Her current publications focus on African, African-American, and Caribbean women writers. She is currently exploring similarities in the writings and in the struggles of women writers from the so-called Third World.

Jane Plastow is Professor of African Theatre and director of the Leeds University Centre for African Studies at the University of Leeds in the UK. She is both an academic and a theater practitioner. She has lived and worked in a range of African nations, including Eritrea, Ethiopia, Gambia, Sudan, Tanzania, and Zimbabwe. She works as both a theater director and in the area of Theater for Development, training activists and working with marginalized communities to enable them to use performance as a means of community empowerment. As an academic she has written widely on African and community-based theater with titles such as *African Theatre and Politics*, *African Theatre: Women*, and *Theatre and Empowerment*.